Kermit Schafer's
BLUNdeRFuL WoRLd of BLooPeRs

Kermit Schafer's
BLUNdeRFUL WORLd
oF BLooPeRs

Foreword by Mike Douglas

Introduction by Burt Prelutsky, *The Los Angeles Times*
Drawings by Doug Anderson
Guest Cartoonist Bob Dunn

Featuring the **TV Blooper Girls,**
Illustrated by Pete Anderson

Fully Indexed

BOUNTY BOOKS
A Division of Crown Publishers, Inc., New York

DEDICATION

This book is dedicated as a sympathetic tribute to members of the broadcasting industry who have been the victims of Bloopers, in the hope that it offers consolation and proof of the fact that they are not alone.

To err is human,
To forgive, divine.
Alexander Pope

To forgive is human,
To err, divine.
Kermit Schafer

CONTENTS

RADIO AND TELEVISION BLOOPERS

- QUIZ PROGRAMS
- KID SHOWS
- SOAP OPERAS
- NEWS
- SPECIAL EVENTS
- SPORTS
- CELEBRITIES
- POLITICS
- ANNOUNCERS
- ACTORS
- DISK JOCKEYS

FOREWORD

When Kermit Schafer appeared on my show I cried. I cried with joy over the funniest segment we ever did—Kermit's presentation of Bloopers.

What impressed me most about Kermit's long-time endeavor to gather broadcasting's funniest mistakes was the fact that no one is immune to these lip slippers. When they happen there's nothing to do but accept them. There's no cure for blooperitis. There is a partial remedy—tape.

While tape has been great for programming, it does, honestly, take some of the spontaneity out of entertainment; with the unused portions of a show also goes the blooper—on to the editing room floor.

Thankfully, though, Kermit Schafer came along 25 years ago to preserve the goofs of our generation for prosperity—oops! I mean posterity.

To Kermit Shafer, thanks for helping us all learn to laugh at ourselves.

Mike Douglas

INTRODUCTION

" UNBLEEPED BLOOPERS "

Burt Prelutsky

Reprinted from The Los Angeles Times

The year 1952 doesn't seem so long ago until you realize that Truman was then President, there was a war going on in Korea, next to nobody had yet heard of Paul Newman, Elvis Presley, Arnold Palmer, Audrey Hepburn or a place called Vietnam, and Gunsmoke was still just the name of a radio show.

In the election of 1952, the team of Eisenhower and Nixon trounced Stevenson and Sparkman. Frank Sinatra's first comeback was still a year off, Martin and Lewis were still hanging together and Liz Taylor was only married to No. 2, Michael Wilding.

When you realize how drastically the world has changed, one way and another, during those past 22 years, the most amazing Kermit Schafer's accomplishment appears. For it was in 1952 that Schafer came up with the notion of collecting and marketing bloopers. When you think of all the fads that have come and gone during that period, it is astounding to realize that Schafer's brainstorm is still going strong after 30 record albums, a dozen books and, now, a movie, "Pardon My Blooper."

The first classic blooper is attributed to Harry Von Zell. In introducing our 31st President to a radio audience, Von Zell called him Hoobert Heever. The latest, according to Schafer, was the TV newscaster who attributed a Washington rumor to "high White Horse souses."

I asked Schafer how he had prepared himself for such a peculiar career. "I was a TV producer for many years. In fact, I produced TV's first full-hour musical for NBC. It starred Ray Heatherton and June Havoc, had a cast of 40 singers and dancers, and a total budget of $300.

"Later, I did some work with Allen Funt. Also, I produced the Rube Goldberg Show in New York. It was on that show and not, as most people think, on Studio One, that Betty Furness did the famous Westinghouse commercial in which she couldn't open the refrigerator door."

I wondered if the fact that live TV is pretty much passe has made the blooper business more difficult. "Not really. I've had very good luck being able to latch on to out-takes. And because everything is taped or filmed, performers feel they can take greater liberties. They feel that if they goof or get tongue-tied, it can always be edited out."

I asked Schafer whether, 25,000 bloopers later, he was beginning to weary of the career he had carved out for himself back in '52. "Never. It's a great life. I help make people laugh and I make a very good living doing it. What more could a person want?" Fame?

But is it enough to have been the fellow who turned slips of the tongue into a profitable way of life? What, I asked Schafer, would he ultimately wish as his epitaph? "I never really gave it any thought. My credo, however, is: To forgive is human; to err, divine."

Let's face it, Schafer has gone on thriving long after such 1952 biggies as Pinky Lee, Korla Pandit, Johnny Ray and Julius La Rosa have been remaindered as trivia items. Bloopers have survived coonskin caps, blue suede shoes and even Tom Swifties. Of everything, in fact, that existed in 1952 the only things that remain basically unaltered and intact today, besides bloopers, are Alabama's Sen. John Sparkman, the American Legion, What's My Line? and David Cassidy's singing voice. Viewed from that perspective, Schafer's contribution to our culture and our society emerges as positively awe-inspiring.

BLUNDERFUL WORLD OF BLOOPERS

Hell to the Chief

The best-known Blooper in my collection of unintended indis-
cretions before microphone and camera is the legendary classic
moment when veteran announcer Harry Von Zell introduced
President Herbert Hoover in early-day radio thusly, "Ladies
and Gentlemen . . . the President of the United States . . .
Hoobert Heever!"

Pick Me Up

On New Year's Eve, Johnny Carson's "Tonight Show" participated in NBC-TV festivities, which included mobile unit
pickups from the Times Square area. In the spirit of the
evening Johnny told his viewers, "We now switch you to
42nd Street and Broadway for a Times Square pickup."

A Slip on the Ice

In a recent weather report which described the snowfall in
the Northwest, the announcer on KHAR, Alaska, said: "And
Helena got six inches during the night . . . Helena, Montana,
that is!"

Really Big

NEWSCASTER: "Beautiful Raquel Welch has won the Inter-
State Theatre Star of the 60's Award and the 1967 Interna-
tional Star of the Year from Cinerama and Pacific Theatres.
Miss Welch is the proud owner of two really big ones."

Family Planning

COMMERCIAL: "So, remember . . . Goodyear four-ply rubber to help prevent families . . . I mean Goodyear rubber tires
to help your family prevent accidents!"

1

Horse Opera

The following commercial was heard over a Philadelphia radio station: "You already know of Aquarama in Philadelphia and the fine entertainment they have there. But I want to tell you of a spectacular they are having on this coming Friday night. For the first time in history, I repeat, for the first time in history . . . see a man rape a horse! Oh, my goodness! I'm sorry . . . for the first time in history see a man race a porpoise . . . Uncle Philsie will be there if he can make it after this."

Father Knows Best

At one point during the coverage of the Republican National Convention which originated from Miami Beach, Florida, a TV camera was taking candid shots of delegates who were in the audience. The camera singled out a very pregnant lady in the audience who was spotted standing directly in front of a large poster which read, "NIXON IS THE ONE!"

No Comment

An announcer, reading it right off the wire: "A severe storm hit Atlantic City, New Jersey, today, bringing high winds, hail, and more than two inches of rain. A sailor was sucked under the boardwalk by a big Wave!"

On Thin Ice

Ed Sullivan told about some of the winter sports athletes he was going to have on his show: "Among them will be the world *sholom* champion."

Situation Wanted

The disc jockey of radio station KOLO, Reno, Nevada, announced the next number to be played on his program: "A Hard Man is Good to Find."

Slip of the Tongue

A disk jockey closing up a late music show said, "We've got just enough time to slip into April Stevens."

Everything Is Coming Up Roses

The commercial was usually stated like this: ". . . So, try Rosedale's flavor of the month, strawberry ripple ice cream." But when the announcer picked it up to read it, this is what the radio listeners heard: ". . . So, try Rosedale's *monthly flavor*, strawberry ripple ice cream."

Good Night, Ladies

In Northbay, Canada, a radio announcer opened his morning show "To the Ladies" by saying, "And now, this number I dedicate to all you newlyweds." He played: "It Only Hurts for a Little While."

Water Boy

The following was heard on a Sacramento, California, FM radio station: "This mellowed beer is brewed with pukey mountain water . . . *pure* Rocky Mountain water!"

Love at First Sight

When I appeared with Merv Griffin as the guest on his new late-night show on CBS-TV, Merv related this blooper on the air. "On the first day of my new afternoon show, I couldn't wait to see who our first sponsor was. It turned out to be a well-known laxative. I eagerly said, 'Well . . . we're off and running.' "

Full Moon Shot

ANNOUNCER: "Stay tuned to NBC for the Apollo *Luny* Landing! . . . *LUNAR!*"

Small Talk

"We will return to the story of the Seven Dwarfs after a pause for a short sponsor's message."

Another First

Christiaan Barnard, prominent surgeon, is here to address a medical convention about his now-famous rear transplant . . . of course . . . I mean *rare* transplant."

Hooked

"See a CBS special on marijuana . . . get the habit, stay tuned to this channel."

Quick on the Drawers

On "The Newlywed Game," the host asked a husband the question "What one thing did it take your wife a few days to get used to doing after marrying you?"
He thought a while and answered, "Oh, I'd have to say going into my drawers." The audience roared. He then said, "Oh, you know, *dresser* drawers!"

No News Is Good News

A newscaster reported in full detail an automobile accident in which the driver lost control of her car on a curve, crashed through the guardrail, and rolled down a steep embankment. She was understandably shaken by this experience but luckily suffered no serious injuries. At this point, the newscaster enthusiastically related the lady's efforts to climb the embankment and obtain aid. He emphatically announced, "As she reached the highway, she climaxed . . . er, *collapsed!*"

Total Recall

Walter Cronkite was reading the news about Rolls-Royce having a recall campaign, when he said, "Rolls-Royce announced today that it is recalling all Rolls-Royce cars made after 1966 because of faulty nuts behind the steering wheels."

Take Him Over the Coals

On Station CJOH, Ottawa, Canada, during the 11:00 P.M. news, Larry Henderson (the news commentator), talking about the Pope lighting the new fire for Easter, said, "The fire was lit in a brassiere . . . I beg your pardon, I mean *brazier!*"

Double Jeopardy

Art Fleming of "Jeopardy" should have been awarded a medal for composure for his recent stone-faced performance on this one: In question to the answer "A decorative section of the bowsprit on sailing vessels," a young lady replied, "What is a maidenhead?"

Small Kraft Warning

Announcer Ed Herlihy blooped: "Another delicious combination for these hot days, also by Kraft, is a chilled grease sandwich and a choke!"

Nipped in the Bud

On the last day of "The Merv Griffin Show" for Westinghouse, Merv was introducing fourteen-year-old singer Julie Budd. Talking about old times, Merv came out with this blooper: "Since we discovered Julie when she was twelve, she really developed (*chuckles from audience*). Oh, come on," Merv replied.

For Pete's Sake

NEWSCASTER: "Now, briefly *recrapping* the news . . . On Capitol Hill, G-O-Lee peters . . . ."

For Men Only

PUBLIC SERVICE ANNOUNCEMENT: *"Residents of this city are urged to show up at the County Whore House for their polio shots . . . I beg your pardon, that should read County Court House."*

Ouch!

ANNOUNCER: "This portion of 'Rawhide' is brought to you by Vaseline Petroleum Jelly!"

Sticky Stuff

LOCAL NEWS: "So, remember . . . we want all of you to turn out for the Peter pulling contest at St. Taffy's Church . . . ugh . . . that should be the *taffy* pulling contest at St. *Peter's* Church this Sunday!"

Could Be

This happened during a children's program patterned after what Art Linkletter does when he talks to kids on his television show.

The emcee asked a little second-grade girl what her favorite subject in school was. The little girl replied gym class. When asked what she did in gym class, she said play games and kick balls around. The emcee came back with: "That will come in handy when you are dating."

Fun and Games

The following was heard on KNOW Radio in Austin, Texas. A sportscaster, while preparing to announce the baseball scores, said . . . "And now, for the gay dames—I mean—the *day's games.*"

Hard Line

Heard on the TV soap opera "As the World Turns": "Yes, sir, he is very long to get a hard with . . . hard to get along with."

Chinese Yen

LOCAL NEWS: "And still missing in the unsolved Bache robbery is a million dollars worth of blue chop sticks!"

Nature in the Raw

On Art Linkletter's kid show, he asked a little girl what she would buy if she had ten dollars. This was her reply. "I would buy my parents some pajamas, because they sleep together without any clothes on!"

Are You Smoking More and Enjoying It Less?

Mel Allen, ace sportscaster, interviewed an all-America football player on his program following the Pabst Blue Ribbon fights on CBS. Mel always made a habit of offering his sponsor's cigars to his guests. However, the football great threw Mel a curve when he pushed a box of cigars aside and said, "I never touch those things, they make me sick!"

So I Ain't Neat

INTERVIEWER: "Doris Day, I've seen your new picture 'Young At Heart,' and I think it's simply wonderful!"
DORIS DAY: "That's great, except we haven't even started shooting, 'Young At Heart' yet!"

That's the Living End

On WHAT'S MY LINE?, Dorothy Kilgallen, famous columnist, introduced a guest panelist in this classic fashion. "Arlene Francis is on a much-deserved vacation in New England tonight, but she left part of her behind, Martin Gabel!"

Ben Who?

Veteran announcer Ben Grauer was announcing for the NBC symphony. "You have been listening to a program of symphonic music by the New York Philharmonic orchestra under the baton of Atosco Touranini . . . ah . . . Otosco Tiscanini . . . that's Arturo Toscanini. Well. Your announcer has been Ben Grauer, ladies and gentlemen. Remember the name—you may never hear it again!"

Dark Victory

On a post-game telecast at San Diego, Los Angeles Dodger announcer Jerry Doggit was talking to Wes Parker who won the ball game on a triple. All of a sudden the lights went out. Jerry said, "Hey, Buzzie, turn the lights on, we didn't mean it. Oh, well, I guess we'll have to do our thing in the dark!"

Rhodes Scholar

Governor James A. Rhodes and President Johnson helped Ohio University in Athens observe its 160th anniversary on May 7, 1964. Governor Rhodes got tangled up on the word "heartily" and said "heartedly." This apparently threw his next phrase. He intended to say this "venerable institution," but it came out "this *venereal* institution."

Half Time

STATION BREAK: "We will reurn to the third half of 'The Virginian' in just a moment."

Coming Up Next!

Public Service Announcement! The following went out on all fifty thousand glorious watts: ". . . To qualify for President Johnson's All American Team, all you have to do is perform a series of sit-ups, push-ups, and *throw-ups!*"

Blue Monday

Scene: "The Garry Moore Show" (in the morning) about five years ago.
Animal-man Ivan T. Sanderson has brought in a gopher and has delivered his spiel. Garry is attempting to get the gopher to perform in some manner—to rear upon its hind legs. Finally, Garry resorts to lifting the gopher's tail and blowing air on its fanny, trying to rouse it to action. Garry blurts out: "What a way to spend a Monday morning—blowing a gopher!"

Time to Retire

The long hours of the Apollo moon landing began to tell on veteran newsman Walter Cronkite when he told his millions of viewers that "Blast-off was scheduled at 11:00 P.OFF . . P.M.!"

The Eyes of Texas

NEWSCASTER: "These Federal funds are being used in the United States, also in Texas."

For Pete's Sake

On a Joey Bishop show Sammy Davis, Jr., and Peter Lawford came on to plug their movie *Salt and Pepper*. When it came time to show a film clip of the movie, Joey announced, "And now for a few scenes from the new movie *Salt and Peter!*" Everyone broke up, including Joey.

Pained Remark

On the Pocket Billiards show "Ten-Twenty," one of the contestants wished to have the billiard balls set up. Joe Wilson, describing the action, said: "At this point Mr. Crane asks the referee to rack his balls!"

Real George

On "This Morning," an ABC conversation program, host Dick Cavett's guest was Christine Jorgenson (once George Jorgenson), who was discussing her transferal of sexes. She explained that there were eight or more different places in the body where sex is determined. "Sex is not determined by genitals alone."

Whereupon the host came out with, "I don't quite think I grasp that . . . I'm sorry, that's an awful thing to say." The entire studio broke up with laughter.

Take Me Out to the Ball Game

The following occurred on "The Yankee Wrap-up," following the New York–Baltimore game. Jerry Coleman was interviewing two of the ballplayers' wives; he was curious about how the family functioned when the husbands are on the road.

WIFE: When he's away, I have to take charge of everything. I have to be pretty much the man in the family.

COLEMAN: Yes, I suppose you do have to wear the pants in the family at that time.

WIFE: Yes, but when he comes home, I take them off.

True or False

Allen Ludden on "Password" asked Juliet Prowse which imitation in her night club act she liked the most.

"Mae West," was Juliet's reply.

Allen remarked that she wore a padded dress for this, which looks very realistic. "But it's not the Juliet I know," Allen commented (*audience laughter*).

"Oh, really?" asked Juliet.

Hoof and Mouth Disease

NEWSCASTER: "And from London we learn that Beatle Ringo Starr is in hospital for an operation on his toenails . . . I believe that should be *tonsils*."

Color Blind

In Cleveland there was a show called "Bowling for Dollars," and Don Webster was host. Out came his next contestant, a black woman. He introduced her as *Golden Coon!* Instantly, in near panic, he corrected himself and said her name was "Golden Crewn."

Dead Pigeon

FIRST ACTOR: "What are you in jail for? . . . I'm in for petty larceny."
SECOND ACTOR: "I'm in for armed robbery . . . some dirty squeal pigeon stooled on me!"

On the Spot

NEWSCASTER: "This is your eleven o'clock newscaster bringing you an on the pot report . . . I mean on the spot retort. . . . I mean on the tot resort . . . oh well, let's just skip it!"

Things Are Rough All Over

NEWSCASTER: "And here is further news on that rape case. All the victim could tell police officials was that her attacker wore rough levi pants."

Navy Blue

ANNOUNCER: "This is a public service announcement. Attention all student nurses. From Washington comes the announcement that the Navy Department is now giving instructions in special new curses for Navy nurses."

How About That!

Mel Allen was guilty of a blooper during a New York Yankee broadcast. He said, "Remember, tomorrow night is Ladies' Night—just fifty cents for all the ladies."

Unfare Remark

Comedienne Carol Burnett has made it a practice to interview people in her audience as part of her own "Carol Burnett" TV program. On one occasion she chatted with a cab driver who enthusiastically told her and her network TV audience that he "had her in my taxi!"

Virgin Territory

Singer Kaye Stevens, making her first TV appearance on the "Jack Paar" late night show, was obviously very nervous after her debut. Paar asked her if this was truly her first appearance on television, to which she replied, "I was a virgin until I appeared on your program, Mr. Paar!"

All Mixed Up

While talking to people in his studio audience, Steve Allen searched for two girls who had sent a note to him stating that King Size and Regular were in his audience. In asking where they were seated, he said, "While I still remember, where are King Size and Cork Tip?"

As a gift he gave the 5-foot 11-inch girl an electric fan, and the shorter girl a Waring Mixor. He always emphasizes the word mixor, not mixer. He said it was a hand mixor: "It mixes hands so well you can never straighten them . . . they now make mixors for His and Hores!"

Chow

Spacecaster: "Apollo Astronauts Armstrong, Aldrin, and Collins have received a 'go' for lunch . . . *launch!*"

Good Sports

NEWSCASTER: "Miss Lesley Bush of Princeton, New Jersey, and Charlie Hickcox of Phoenix, Arizona, both Olympic Gold Medal winners, will be married Saturday at Bloomington.

"They will spend their honeymoon in an AAU sponsored exhibition in Montevideo, Uruguay."

Girl Talk

"For excitement and beautiful girls see color *cleverage* of the Rose Bowl Game New Year's Day on CBS."

Bedtime Story

On "The Joey Bishop Show," Senator Barry Goldwater had been asked by Joey if he would like to be on the show twice a week. The senator replied, "No, thank you, I'd much rather watch you in bed with my wife."

I Never Remember a Face

ANNOUNCER: "See a TV special—the Russian Bolshoi Ballet in a never-to-be remembered performance Sunday at nine."

Answer Yes or No

David Frost had F. Lee Bailey as his guest. They were discussing Truman Capote's book *In Cold Blood*. David turned to his studio audience, and asked, how many of you read the film or saw the book?

Testy

A newscaster on KFRU in Columbia, Missouri, began a news-cast with this: "Magistrate Judge Temple Morgett set Wednes-day as the final day for lawyers to file their briefs in the case of a local man arrested for drunken driving who refused to take a breast test . . . *breath* test!"

Inspirational Message

Following the sermonette that closed the regular TV programming for the day on a Palm Springs, California, TV station, late viewers were treated to a showing of stag movies that were being screened by a station employee. This engineering blooper resulted in an avalanche of phone calls, many of which requested a rerun of the films.

A Ding a Ling

During one of Steve Allen's shows he kept substituting the word "dingdong" for other words. He had on this particular show a culinary expert to whom Steve said, "The way to a man's heart is through his *dingdong*." It should have been stomach, of course.

Peep Show

During television coverage of a political convention some years ago, NBC-TV was using a new camera called "the creepy peepie" to cover the events on the convention floor. During a station break an announcer on one of our local stations encouraged us to "get full convention coverage with NBC and its creepy *people*."

Call a Cop

On local radio station WAOK in Rhode Island, when a disc jockey was advertising the YMCA Fair, he said, "Children under twelve must be accomplished by an adult . . . uh . . . er . . . that is, children must be *accompanied* by an adult under twelve years of age."

He's Got to Go

Johnny Carson said on "The Tonight Show": "Here's how to relieve an upsex stomach . . . I mean an *upsep* stomach . . . with Sex Lax . . . *Ex-lax!*"

Party Girl

Comedian Marty Ingels appeared as a guest on "The Steve Allen Show." Steve's wife, Jayne Meadows, also appeared on the program. Jayne got all fouled up when she told Steve, "I knew that Marty was the type to have a child . . . I saw him at a party recently [audience laughter] . . . well, you know what I mean."

Sick Commercial

COMMERCIAL: "So try Vick's 44 Cough Syrup and we guarantee that you'll never get any better!"

On the Make

Heard on "What's My Line."
BENNETT CERF: "Is the product made in Hollywood?"
ARLENE FRANCIS: "Isn't everybody?"

Ready Eddy

Ed Sullivan, closing out his Sunday night TV program, found a few seconds to do a quick public service message. He closed his show, "And now a word about tuberculosis . . . Good night, everybody . . . help stamp out *TV!*"

No Comment

NEWSCASTER: ". . . and here is more concerning the Pope's current condition following the surgical removal of his prostate: It has been learned that the fountains in Vatican Square have been ordered turned off because it had been feared that the sound of running water would bother the Pope."

Be My Guest

ANNOUNCER: "Good evening, this is your musicologist, Fred Laney. Tonight's program features music for ancient instruments and sopranos. Tonight's guest is ancient soprano, Viola Finkleoffer."

Burp

NEWSCASTER: "President Johnson and Premier Kosygin are now having luncheon comprising a typical American meal in Gasboro, New Jersey . . . that should be Glassboro . . . and now a word from Alka Seltzer!"

Even Your Best Friend Won't Tell You

ANNOUNCER: "Go to your neighborhood theatre to see Rita Hayworth, whose Salami will take your breath away . . . that should be Salome."

It's Worth a Try

During the Pueblo spy ship crisis NBC news commentator Pauline Fredericks was broadcasting a special U.N. news summary. This summary occurred on a Saturday morning, when many kids shows were pre-empted. She told her viewers that ". . . Canada was helping decide whether the U.N. will send (KIDS SHOW CUT IN) the Cub Scouts!"

Shaggy Dog Story

On the NBC "Today" show, newscaster Merrill Mueller did the commercial lead-in for Alpo Dog Food thus: "I see Hugh Downs is keeping some shady lady lately . . . I mean some shaggy company lately . . . I mean a shaggy dog lately!"

He Must Be Choking

Curt Gowdy, during the broadcast of a World Series game between the Boston Red Sox and the St. Louis Cardinals and also during a football game between the San Diego Chargers and the Oakland Raiders, observed: "Folks, this is perfect weather for today's game. Not a breath of air."

Just Reward

Comedians Don Rickles and Red Buttons appeared as guests on the "Mike Douglas Show." Rickles was singing the praises of a Danny Thomas-produced program entitled "Zero Man." In his enthusiasm for the program Rickles inadvertently said, "I wouldn't be a bit surprised if Danny Thomas got an Enema Award for this one."

He's Working on a New Case

NEWSCASTER: "Stay tuned to ABC-TV's 'Good Company' celebrity interview program, starring F. Lee Bailey, prominent lawyer known throughout the bars of the nation."

So What Else Is New?

On the Bob and Ray Show of several years ago Ray had on an apron as he was demonstrating how to make a fancy octopus salad. He had the body of an octopus before him and as he laid the carrot curls around it he said, ". . . and these, ladies, are the testicles!" *SILENCE . . . SILENCE . . . AND MORE SILENCE.*

Fair Enough

WEATHER FORECST: "This is your weather girl bringing you the forecast for eastern Texas and vicinity, direct from the airport. Today's forecast is for fair and mild with a pleasant weekend in prospect for you golfers and fishermen. (LOUD CLAP OF THUNDER) Oh, oh . . . you had better bring your rubbers."

The Rain In Spain

During a roundtable TV discussion that centered around *My Fair Lady* one of the participants said that the climax of the play occurred when the stars decided to marry. Others said that it occurred earlier. The moderator, in pointing out that the climax was seen earlier in the play, mentioned that the marriage was really anticlimactic, then added, "Don't think that I mean that marriage is an anticlimax, there are many climaxes in marriage (FLUSTERED) . . . well, that is . . . well, I am sure that you all know what I mean."

A Lot of Guts

SPORTSCASTER: "Davis Cup Tennis Star Fred Perry severely sprained his leg and it is feared that he might have served a nerve, I mean, severed!"

Hostess with the Mostest

Oleg Cassini did the commentary on a fashion show he presented on Johnny Carson's "The Tonight Show." He described a gown worn by one of his models in this way: "This is a lovely hostess dinner dress with a very low neckline for easy entertaining."

The Old Gray Mare

A youngster told Art Linkletter that he watched a milkman's parked horse for a while and figured out that the animal was stuck because "it just lost all of its gasoline."

Doctor Cronkite

CBS newscaster Walter Cronkite blooped the following: "Prayers were offered throughout the world as Pope Paul planned for prostate surgery at the Pentagon . . . that should be the Vatican."

Oh God-Frey

Heard on the Arthur Godfrey morning radio show on CBS: "This is truly a fine product for the relief of aches and pains, so for all of you who find it stiff in the morning, try Bufferin."

All Wet

In one of his traditional introductions of celebrities in his audience Ed Sullivan asked swimming champions Johnny Weismuller and Buster Crabbe to take a bow, after which he told his nationwide audience that ". . . these two fine gentlemen are being put into the Swimming Hole of Fame."

Don't Miss It If You Can

ANNOUNCER: " 'Tuesday Night at the Movies' will be seen on Saturday of this week instead of Monday."

I Love Lucy

DISC JOCKEY: ". . . continuing now with more music from the album *'Mr. Lucy Goes Latin'* . . . that should be *Mr. Lucky* . . . we hear a selection "Coffee Bells and Cow Beans" . . . I mean "Cow Bells and Coffee Beans" as performed by Henry Mancini and his swinging organ."

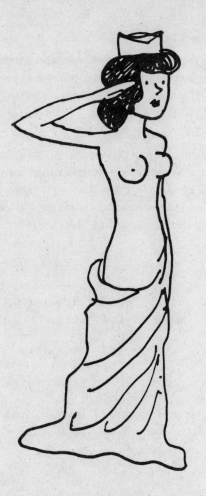

At Ease

QUIZ MASTER: "All right, young lady, before we ask you your
first question, what branch of service are you in?
CONTESTANT: I am a Wave.
QUIZ MASTER: My, you must be proud to wear your uniform.
Tell me . . . what is the first thing you are taught as a Wave?
CONTESTANT: One of the first things we learned is, before we
do anything to disgrace our uniforms, we should take them
off."

Picket March

COMMENTATOR: ". . . and as Labor leader George Meany made his way to the speaker's stand the band struck up 'Stars and Strikes Forever.'"

Ready Eddie

NEWSCASTER: "It was reported that Connie Stevens was about to give birth to a child. When questioned, Eddie Fisher would not comment about the impending blessed event. This report was verified by a source believed responsible."

Miss-Take

Heard on Hy Gardner's Miami television program: "It has been erroneously reported that Christine Jorgenson is flat-busted."

Pitch Man

SPORTSCASTER: "Here is a sports bulletin just received from the news room. It is now official! Juan Pizzaro has just pissed a no hit-no run ball game!"

Beauty and the Beast

Johnny Carson had five Miss America contestants as guests on his program, as well as other guests. He referred to them in this fashion: ". . . and on our show tonight we have five Miss America contestants and also some dogs (AUDIENCE ROARS) . . . I mean real dogs (MORE AUDIENCE LAUGHTER) . . . come on, now, you know I mean dogs that bark!"

Cat-Astrophic

MOVIE COMMERCIAL: " 'Saturday at the Movies' brings you another hit motion picture. See Elizabeth Taylor and Paul Newman together in a *Cot on a Hot Tin Roof.*"

Family Show

Arlene Francis asked a young lady whose occupation was being guessed on "What's My Line" if she worked for a nonprofit organization. Emcee John Daly consulted with her for a moment and then told the panel: "I must warn you that there is a hooker here."

Father of Our Country

STATION BREAK: "Stay tuned for 'Peyton Place,' where today you will meet Dr. Michael Rossi, who is responsible for most of the children born in this small country town."

Yes, We Have No Bananas

WIOD, Miami, disc jockey Tom Gauger tells about the announcer who blooped, "Metropolitan Opera star Anna Moffo will now sing 'The Star-Spangled Banana.' "

Good Night!

"This is Art Linkletter saying good night . . . and a special thanks to you, Edith Head, and your girls for bringing your dresses down on our program."

Break Bread

When Durwood Kirby devoted the CBS "Dimension" radio program to Kermit Schafer's Blooper book entitled *Prize Bloopers,* he recalled the time he announced the opening of a radio program thusly: "The Blonde Bed Breakers are on the air! . . . I mean *The Bond Bread Bakers!*"

Miss Conception

In the 1965 Miss America Beauty Pageant the emcee was back-stage talking to the five semifinalists while the judges were choosing Miss America, when he came up with this Blooper: "Have you ever seen five more expectant young ladies?"

For You, Deefeecult

On Johnny Carson's "The Tonight Show" a collector of butterflies was Johnny's guest. When Johnny was shown some handsome frames that displayed the butterflies under glass, Johnny asked, "How do you mount a butterfly? It must be very difficult."

He's a Big One!

Johnny Carson during a lead-in for a Jolly Green Giant commercial looked into a camera and said, "Have you ever walked out of your house and found yourself face to face with a huge green fruit?"

Red Face

On the "Red Skelton Show" a few years ago Red was talking about root beer; he suggested to his viewers that they drink plenty of root beer because "it is good for your root." It took the audience quite a while to get over that one!!

Air Sick

Frank McGee, NBC News, gave this information to the viewing public during the course of a Gemini space flight: "I have just learned that we do have the film of the astronauts' breakfast, which should be coming up shortly."

Wrong Channel

DISC JOCKEY: ". . . . and here now is another million seller sung by popular Urethra Franklin . . . *Aretha!*"

Saucy Commercial

"So look for Hunt's tomato sauce on your favorite grocer's can . . . *shelf!*"

Good Deed for the Day

LOCAL NEWS: "The Girl Scouts in this area are planning to form a Little Mothers Club much like the already formed Little Fathers Club headed by their scout master. All Girl Scouts interested in becoming 'little mothers' are to meet with the Boy Scout Master in the high school gym after this meeting."

You Only Hurt the One You Love

DISC JOCKEY: "We hear now the horny sound of Al Hirt . . . I mean the horny horn of Al Hirt . . . the horn sound of Al Hirt!!! . . . I'm really sorry, Al."

Without Rhyme or Reasoner

"This is Harry Reasoner reminding you to tune in this Sunday when CBS-TV will prevent the Johnson wedding!"

Elementary, My Dear Watson

NEWSCASTER: "The battered bodies of the two young women, both clad in black bathing suits, were found by fishermen Friday night in a canal off the Intracoastal Waterway, a quarter of a mile north of the Dania Beach Boulevard bridge. The younger girl had been shot fatally and her companion, believed to be Mrs. Frank, was killed from a blow on the back of the head with a sharp object—possibly an ax. Both had fractured skulls from blows on the back of the head, and both of the attractive young women were stabbed in the upper abdomen. Their bodies were tied around the neck with electrical cord to two concrete blocks . . . . Police suspect foul play!"

A Smash

"Here is a bulletin from NBC News . . . Newark, New Jersey . . . Militant Civil Rights leaders, angered by the presence of newsmen at their meeting, smashed cameras and TV equipment . . . and now back to 'Beat The Press' . . . er . . . *'Meet The Press'!*"

A Hot Number

COMMERCIAL: "So stop by our downtown store and visit our fashion center. You will see our lovely models in heat . . . (PAUSE, TURNS PAGE) . . . resistant fabrics which will keep you cooler this summer."

Dead Men Tell No Tales

PUBLIC SERVICE ANNOUNCEMENT: "So when you drive, be sure to keep a safe distance from the car in front of you; tail-getting will get you nowhere . . . that should be tail-gating."

A Nose for News

NEWSCASTER: ". . . and now for some nose newts!"

He Lipths

On the "Mike Douglas Show" Mike was having a discussion with Sheila MacRae and a well-known children's doctor. Mike asked: "Doctor, is it dangerous to thuck your sumb?"

The Story of Peter Pan

COMMERCIAL: ". . . and so, ladies, on your next trip to your grocer be sure to order Peanut Pan Peter Butter."

Sacrilegous Song

ANNOUNCER: ". . . and now our guest soloist, Marian Anderson, will sing Gounod's 'Oyvey Maria.' "

Help!

Curt Gowdy dropped this classic during the broadcast of the AFL All-Star Game. Noting that a downpour had formed a small lagoon on the field of play, he remarked: "If there's a pileup there, they'll have to give some of the players artificial insemination."

I'd Rather Fight

COMMERCIAL: "So be among the many who change over to mild-tasting Phillies cigars. Remember . . . all the fellas are switching to Fellas . . . I mean Phillies."

News Leak

"Be sure to attend the Elks' Club Charity Beer Drinking Contest with entry fees going to charity. The beer drinking contest starts Wednesday afternoon with eliminations all day Thursday."

Say It Isn't So!

On "You Don't Say" daytime program the emcee has two lights on the panel in front of him that flash the contestants' score. Once when one of the lights conked out, he looked down and said, "Hey, my little thing isn't working!" The audience roared. After the laughter died down, he looked at guest panelist Vincent Price and said, "Don't you say one word!"

I Wish I Was Single Again

On a David Susskind "Open End" TV program, a birth control authority was his invited guest, who told viewers "that a birth control experiment is soon to start at a single clinic (AUDIENCE TITTERS) . . . by a single clinic, I don't mean for people who are single!"

Oh, Oh

When Art Linkletter interviewed columnist Hedda Hopper on his "Talent Scouts" show, the discussion drifted to old stars of yesteryear. Linkletter asked Hopper how she thought today's crop of actors stacked up against the likes of Douglas Fairbanks, Sr. She replied, "Sean Connery is the closest." Art said, "Oh, you mean 007? . . . Yes, he fixes everybody." Hedda snapped back with: "Yes, and he especially fixes the girls!"

Kentucky Bourbon

SPORTSCASTER: "For western Kentucky, All-American Bobby Rascoe was high with twenty-seven pints!"

Born Yesterday

Virginia Graham, femcee of her "Girl Talk" TV show on NBC, had screen actress Angie Dickinson as her guest, who told of her recently born child. Miss Graham asked, "How old was she when she was born?"

Livid Color

When Lana Turner was a mystery guest on "What's My Line," the question came around to Bennett Cerf. He asked if she was best known as a pin-up girl. Miss Turner said, "No." John Daly interrupted, saying, "Well, actually, that's a broad question." After the audience laughter had subsided, John Daly said, "I thank God we are not in color, I haven't blushed in twenty years!"

Baby Talk

Nancy Dickerson, NBC news commentator, was describing the events surrounding the birth of President Johnson's first grandchild. The TV station accidentally cut off the word *cigars* from her last news item detailing this happy event, with the following result: "Lucy's husband, Pat Nugent, when he learned of the blessed event, passed out . . ."

Duped

Ralph Renick, WTVJ, Miami, news director and commentator, was reaching the end of one of his strongly worded editorials. The subject was waste in government. He paused to let the facts sink in and then said in measured tones, "We must do away with this dupeless needication."

Girl Watchers

NEWSCASTER: "Mayor John Lindsay said he will keep an eye on the topless situation in New York; he further said that the courts will also take a close look at the girls."

Lest We Forget

Maggie McNellis interviewed a famous screen personality on her "Luncheon at the Latin Quarter" program. She told the audience of the great unforgettable motion picture her guest starred in and, for the world of her, couldn't think of what it was about.

She Sells Sea Shells

Former Miss America Bess Meyerson, describing the beauty pageant, told of the bathing beauties spending the day taking pictures on the broad walk at the she shore in Atlantic City.

Fish Story

On the popular TV cooking program "The French Chef," featuring Julia Child, the following was heard: "It's best to go to the fish market early Friday morning and leave your odor."

Give the Girl a Handout

Ed Sullivan, introducing a guest in his audience, blooped the following: "Sitting out in our audience is talented Dolores Gray, currently starving on Broadway."

Order, Please

When Pope Paul visited this country, he stayed at Cardinal Spellman's residence in New York. NBC's Bill Ryan, who described this momentous visit, told the TV millions that "Pope Paul has just left Cardinal Spellman's restaurant . . . . er, residence . . . . after having a bite to eat, for Yankee Stadium."

Curtain Time

On PLAY YOUR HUNCH, starring Merv Griffin as emcee, there were three men shown, to stump the contestants. Each one had a pole in his hand with the upper part obscured by a curtain. On only one of these poles, a mason's hod was balanced. Merv said, "Now to score another point, can you tell me which one of these men has a hod on his pole!"

The Last Roundup

A news director at WORL in Boston started each morning with a twenty-five-minute news roundup. His first story on this particular morning came out, "Police in Danvers this morning discovered the half-nude body of a man lodged in a sewer pipe. Although not believed to be connected to the current rash of gangland slayings, police have termed the death a sewercide."

Bungles for Britain

While in London I was listening to the BBC, and I heard what I thought was a classic blooper on a TV station featuring a dramatic program depicting the Battle of Britain during World War II. I ran for my notebook when I heard the actress say to her soldier boyfriend, "I know everything will be all right, if you will only keep your pecker up." It wasn't until some time later that I discovered that "pecker" meant courage.

Humpty Bumpty

Wire service typos are very often responsible for newscasters' goofs, especially when news is read "cold" right off the ticker. Here is an example of a newsman's reading an Associated Press news item that was handed to him which he was on the air and which was broadcast over KFRB, Alaska. "A secretary who humped her boss caused more than five thousand dollars in damages. . . . Er, I'm sure they must have meant 'Bumped into her boss!' "

Congratulations

On "The Today Show," newsman Lem Tucker told about: "Lynda Bird Robb who had a little baby girl shortly after midwife . . . *midnight!*"

Swan Song

During a coast-to-coast broadcast of the Metropolitan Opera on ABC, Lauritz Melchior, distinguished tenor of the Met, was singing the leading role in *Lohengrin*. In the last act he was supposed to leave the stage in a boat drawn by swans; however, the swans missed the cue of the stage crew and left the stage while Melchior was still singing. In complete calm, he turned to his fellow performers and said: "What time does the next swan leave?"

Watch Your P's and Q's

COMMENTATOR: "Ronald Reagan was expected to make a personal pee to the G.O.Plee Platform Committee."

Doin' What Comes Naturally

On the Johnny Carson show the following situation came up: Johnny was interviewing Helen and Frank Beardsley of California, parents of 20 children. Johnny asked how do you manage, having 20 children? Mrs. Beardsley replied, "I'm doing what I enjoy most, I guess I was just made for it."

The audience went wild. After they left, Johnny said, "I only have three children, I don't know how they do it." Someone from the audience hollered, *"Oh, yes you do!"*

Beat Me, Daddy

WEATHER FORECASTER: "Well, folks, it's raining again . . . and the sun is shining. I've heard it said that when it rains when the sun is out, the Devil is beating his wife. It looks like he's been banging her . . . that is, beating her, all week."

Heaven Can Wait

Seen on Art Linkletter's "House Party": LINKLETTER: "Do you have any pets?" LITTLE GIRL: "No, I did have a fish but he died." LINKLETTER: "And it went to fish heaven?" LITTLE GIRL: "No, I threw him down the toilet."

Frank Question, Frank Answer

A youngster, when being interviewed during intermission in a Montreal-New York Hockey Game, was asked this question by Frank Selky, Jr.:

"Did you have a nice Christmas?"

"No."

"Why?"

"I'm Jewish!"

Having a Ball

Lucille Ball appeared as a guest on the new "Virginia Graham Show." Also appearing as a guest was a magician, who was displaying his remarkable sleight-of-hand tricks with little disappearing balls. At one point of his act he told Lucille, "You think I have two balls," to which she replied, "I hope so!"

Give Him a Hand

A new disc jockey was understandably nervous his first day on the air. His assignment was to "break" a new Beatles record. This was the result: "Here is the next number one record by the Beatles: 'I Want to Hold Your Gland . . . *Hand!*'"

The Birds and the Bees

Singer Pat Boone appeared as a guest cohost on "The Mike Douglas Show." Pat brought with him his wife, Shirley, and his four daughters, who sang on the program. When Mike probed into Pat's married life, he asked if Shirley traveled with him, to which Pat replied, "It seemed that my wife Shirley was always pregnant until we found out what was causing it. . . . I mean—" (The audience laughter continued into the next commercial, and viewers never did find out what he meant.)

A Great Pair

SPECIAL EVENTS: The following blooper occurred when beautiful Raquel Welch was called upon to make an Academy Award presentation: "My name is Raquel Welch. . . . I am here for visual effects" (*Audience laughter*) "And I have two of them. (*More Laughter.*) I mean nominations for *Marooned* and *Krakatoa, East of Java!*"

Aces Wild

A radio station in Seattle, Washington, broadcasts the Super-Sonics basketball games. A sponsor of these games is Richfield Products and Credit Cards. A hapless announcer was expounding on the virtues of the Richfield credit card when this popped out: "Yessiree folks, Richfield credit cards are like an ass in the hole (*Gulp.*) So why don't you keep one up your . . . (*Gulp*) uh . . . sleeve!"

Prune Bowl

ANNOUNCER: "See color cleverage of all the major college bowel games New Year's day on NBC."

Holy Cow!

Herb Rau, Miami news columnist, reported the following, which occurred on a Channel 6, Miami, newscast: "An announcer talked about one of the FBI's most wanted criminals and on the screen, inadvertently, we hope, flashed a picture of Pope Paul."

Double Meaning

Jack Paar, always known for coming out with the unpredictable, introduced movie star Jayne Mansfield thus: "And here they are . . . Jayne Mansfield!"

No Bunk

A hillbilly singer, Cecil Gill, was scheduled to sing, "There's An Empty Cot in the Bunk House Tonight." The announcer fluffed "Cecil Gill, the Yodeling Country Boy, will now sing, 'There's An Empty Bunk in the Cathouse Tonight.' "

Flying High

Larry King, popular radio and TV personality, broadcasting the color during the telecast of the Miami Dolphins–Baltimore Colts football game, observed: "Now coming onto the field to entertain the fans is the Air Force Academy Drug and Bugle Corps."

Age Before Beauty

Bob Hope, sponsor of the annual Desert Classic Golf Tournament from Palm Springs, California, was stalling for time while Arnold Palmer and Ray Floyd were out on the golf course playing, sudden death having come into the eighteenth hole in a tie. This was the tournament in which the celebrated Vice President Spiro T. Agnew "beanings" took place. Hope decided to interview the scantily attired Desert Classic girls who acted as scorekeepers. He asked one girl, "How old are you?" "Twenty-four" she replied. "I've got balls older than that," said Hope. Realizing what he had said when he heard the audience surrounding the eighteenth hole roar, he countered with, "Of course, I mean *golf balls!*"

Help!

PUBLIC SERVICE ANNOUNCEMENT: "And now this tip from the American Red Cross. In case of drowning, lay the girl . . . lay the drowning victim on her back and try mouth-to-mouth breeding . . . (GULP) *breathing!*"

Get Out Of Town

News Director Dave Duncan of WLKW, Rhode Island was the victim of this emergency news bulletin: "From his emergency flood headquarters at City Hall, Mayor Friedman has just ordered all families living near or adjacent to the Mill River to ejaculate immediately."

Flipping His Lid

Accepting the Oscar award in behalf of Cliff Robertson, Academy Award winner for the best actor role in *Charlie,* the recipient said that he regretted that Robertson was not present, "as he was *flipping* in the *Filmapinnes.*"

Peep Show

Singer Roberta Sherwood appeared as a guest on a program starring radio and TV personality Bill Goodwin. The conversation got around to Walter Winchell, who discovered Roberta in a small nightclub in Miami.

BILL: "Walter Winchell was there peeking through keyholes?"

ROBERTA: "He wasn't peeking through keyholes."

BILL: "That his racket. They say he looks through peeholes."
     (Audience hysteria.)

Mind Blower

SPONSOR: "I am speaking to you from the National Bowling Championship featuring the nation's top lady blowers . . . bowlers . . . and our next blower is Myrtle Haggarity . . . *bowler!*"

Just Ducky

News director John Nance tells about the time ABC newsman Peter Jennings blooped, "A group of American marines got a good look at how the Vietcong treat their prisoners today in the jungles of South Vietnam. A Marine patrol came across the remains of a small VC prison camp near the jungle highlands village of Fuck Doh . . . that should be Duc Pho."

Out of this World

When Astronaut Wally Schirra appeared as a guest for an interview on "Meet the Press," panelist Lawrence Spivak asked: "How does it feel to be in a state of *wastelessness?*"

A Stopper

An attractive and well-stacked young lady came on "The Virginia Graham Show" to do a commercial, as she had previously done on several TV shows. Comic Dennis Wholey, a guest on the program, quipped, "Here she is again . . . the plug of the week!"

Deuces Wild

SPORTSCASTER: "I'm standing at the rear of the green of the short one hundred forty-five yard par three. With the wind behind them, most of the girl pros easily reached this green with a six or a seven iron. In yesterday's round the wind was blowing in the opposite direction; only one girl had a douche on this hole . . . DEUCE!

By George

On "Name That Tune," emcee George De Witt was desperately trying to give a young lady, who was recently married, the clue to the song title, "I Love You." After she missed the title several times the emcee hinted, "What did you say to your husband on your wedding night?" After a few seconds of thought she replied, "Gosh, that's a hard one."

Billy the Kid

Many of the talk shows have music when it's time for a commercial. David Frost, anticipating just such a moment, observed, "We have to take a break, because I can see Billy is about to tinkle again."

Pay As You Go

COMMERCIAL: "And remember—at People's Credit, you pee whichever way is easiest for you."

Rock Festival

NEWSCASTER: "Good evening. Here are tonight's headlines: 'Nixon Gets Stoned On Trip' . . ."

Honesty is the Best Policy

The TV play was *Abe Lincoln in Illinois* . . . in which Raymond Massey starred. The actors on stage were bidding farewell to the president. . . . When one of them called out . . . "G'bye Mister Massey."

Tongue Twister

NEWSCASTER: "The only way the man could be identified was by the fact that he was standing in the road alongside his stalled automobile with a cool tit in his hand."

Henny Youngman

COMMERCIAL: "Houchens Market has fresh young hens ready for the rooster . . . er . . . roaster."

Falling Stars

Candy Jones, mistress of ceremonies on the TV program YOUR LUCKY STAR on WPIX in New York, told her viewers: "Tonight we are going to find out which Hollywood movie stars were born under the sign of Crappycorn."

Lost in a Fog

WEATHER FORECASTER: "It seems that we haven't had much weather lately . . . for some reason we don't get too much of it this time of year."

Rock and Roll

NEWSCASTER: "Also keeping an eye on the Woodstock Rock Festival was New York's Governor Rockin Nelsenfeller!!!"

Shot-Gun Wedding

On a program entitled "It's Your Move," emanating from Canada, emcee Paul Hanover welcomed back a guest contestant who had missed a few programs as a result of getting married. Hanover innocently asked, "How come you had to go and get married like that?" Her comeback was: "Oh, we didn't *have* to get married!"

Young at Heart

Gig Young appeared as a guest on "The Merv Griffin Show." Gig dwelt on the fact that he is no longer married. Merv innocently asked, "Do you find it hard getting up in the morning since you're a bachelor?"

Get the Picture?

Johnny Carson had Tony Randall as his guest on the "Tonight Show." Johnny asked Tony to read a cue card for his next commercial, Camelon panty hose. Tony read, "and now here's a word about a panty hose that fits almost any man or woman. . . ." While trying to figure that one out, Johnny was holding up a Kodak camera sign. He blurted out, "Now here's a word from Kotex . . . *Kodak.*"

Believe It or Not

The following excerpt is reported verbatim from a live broadcast. The name of the program is "Central Florida Showcase." This question is being asked of Dr. Robert Cade, the inventor of the drink Gatorade: "What did the original drink taste like, doctor?" "The first Gatorade was served to a football team. A player got it. He was a guard at the University who plays with the Steelers now. He got the first drink of Gatorade, took a big swallow, and said, "This stuff tastes like piss!"

Ladies' Day

Hugh Downs had Timothy Leary as his guest on "The Today Show." The discussion centered about Leary's provocative books on habit-forming drugs. Downs interrupted the discussion with, "Before we continue, let's take a look at this type of pot that the ladies will enjoy—*TEFLON!*"

Chick and Double Chick

A television network news commentator, describing the historic Apollo moon landing, observed that "Astronaut Alan Shepard is now going over his chick list before launching."

Hard Question

Heard on the ABC-TV "Newlywed Game." "Couple number three: What Beatle song reminds you of your wedding night?" "It's Been a Hard Day's Night!"

London Fog

When I was in London, I watched TV personality Simon Dee on London's ITV network. Simon Dee conducts a nighttime TV program very similar to Johnny Carson's, Merv Griffin's, and Dick Cavett's in the States. Simon had as his guest Millicent Martin, a popular singer in England. She explained that she was quite nervous that night because her husband, a producer, had a show opening titled, *"Vivat! Vivat! Vagina!*. . . . I mean *Vivat! Vivat! Regina!"*

Dumb Bunny

SPORTSCASTER: Many different kinds of animals have interrupted football games, but perhaps none so unusual as this one: "It's a big hippity-hop rabbit, jacking off down the field."

Of Mice and Men

SPORTSCASTER: "This is Jack Drees bringing you another major PGA Tournament from the White Mouse Country Club in Philadeplhia . . . I'm sorry, that should be White Marsh Country Club."

Small Talk

DISC JOCKEY: "COCM Stereo Land now presents popular Hawaiian favorite Don Ho with Tiny Boobies . . . uh . . . Tiny Bubbles"

My Old Kentucky Home

COMMERCIAL: "So folks, if you are looking for the easy way to enjoy your dinner this Sunday, just drop by the colonel's place for delicious finger lickin' Kenfucky fried chicken."

Is This Any Way to Run an Airline?

When "Playhouse Ninety" was telecast live over the CBS network several years ago, a drama in which a passenger airplane had lost one motor was the theme. The actress portraying a stewardess came up with this line in the excitement of the moment: "Will all passengers pease deplene from the real exit . . . er . . . er . . . will all passengers please pee out the real exit. . . . Thank you."

Can't Believe I Ate . . .

An early-morning DJ did his first commercial. All went well until he tried getting beyond the following portion from the copy department: "You will love this delicious bread. By the way, did you know how the sandwich got its name? The Earl of Sandwich was the first man to put his meat between two pieces of bread."

Food for Thought

Graham Kerr, the emcee of his own delightful cooking show, "The Galloping Gourmet," came up with this classic when he was talking about squid: "A squid, as you know of course, has ten testicles . . . ten *tentacles*. Oh, my gosh!"

Fall Guy

Radio and television interviewers often have difficulty keeping their programs interesting and brisk. Some will very often think ahead to their next question before actually hearing the answer to their previous question, as evidence a portion of this interview:

INTERVIEWER: "Tell us about your recent safari to Africa."
GUEST: "I am sorry to tell you that this particular trip you refer to was canceled when I slipped in my bathroom and suffered a severe brain concussion, and as a result I was hospitalized for eight weeks."
INTERVIEWER: "Really? . . . How wonderful . . . What about your trip to the Congo?"

Watch It!

John Cameron Swayze, veteran newscaster who has become identified with the Timex commercials and their underwater demonstrations, was telling about one of his sponsor's new watches in this fashion. "So when you are in the market for a perfect gift, may we *rewind* you about Timex."

Thanks a Lot

NEWSCAST: "This is DIMENSION, Allen Jackson reporting on the CBS Radio Network from New York. Today's big news story is the national spreading of the flu epidemic . . . brought to you by the Mennen Company!"

To the Rear, March!

ANNOUNCER: "And now the band will pay a tribute to the rear of Senator Barry Goldwater!!"

Asleep in the Deep

WEATHER FORECASTER: "The six A.M. forecast is for partly croudy with a seventy-five percent chance of rain mixed with sleep early this morning."

Fly Now, Play Later

Dan Rowan of "Laugh In" appeared with Dick Cavett on his late night program. Rowan seemed to be bothered by a fly during the course of his interview. Dick kept kidding him about the pest, and at one point he said, "After station break, we'll talk about your fly."

While Burns Roams

On the Johnny Carson TONIGHT SHOW, George Burns told Rosemary Clooney that after 38 years, singing is all he can do. He then asked Rosemary . . . "How come you and José Ferrer have five children?" to which she replied "José doesn't sing!" "Oh, he does it the hard way," Burns snapped back.

To the Rear

Faye Emerson, on the Arthur Godfrey TV program, bloopered the following: "Walter Slezak, whenever I think of you, I think of your Fanny . . . Of course I mean your starring role in *Fanny!*"

Double Trouble

QUIZ EMCEE: "All right now, for a twenty-five-dollar savings bond, you have fifteen seconds to name as many things as you can that come in pairs."
CONTESTANT: "Let's see . . . shoes . . . gloves . . . er, *brassieres!*"

Special Elections

COMMENTATOR: "And from France comes word that action will not be taken on this important matter until after their general erections!"

Just Peachy

David Brinkley, during the description of former Congresswoman Rankin's unprecedented protest trip to Washington, told his viewers that ". . . accompanying Miss Rankin are 5,000 women peach marchers."

Simple Arithmetic

On an interview program conducted by Johnny Olsen, a young lady was asked her age. She made it a point to emphasize that she was twenty-one years old. When she was asked what she was doing in New York, she replied, "Oh, I'm here with my parents . . . they are celebrating their twentieth anniversary today."

Good Show

On ABC's WIDE WORLD OF SPORTS, emcee Jim McKay was describing the World Barrel-Jumping Championship, and came out with this classic. "Leo Lebel has been competing with a pulled stomach muscle, showing a lot of guts!"

Johnny on the Spot

In the televised description of an important PGA golf tournament, the following was heard: "And now Johnny Tee is on the pot . . . of course I mean John Pott is on the tee!"

When You Gotta Go

POLITICAL RALLY: "And now, moments before the polling of the delegates officially starts, I see Representative West making his way to the rest room . . . I beg your pardon . . . Representative West is making his way to the rostrum!!!"

Nuts to You

COOKING PROGRAM: "Good morning. Today we are going to bake a spice cake, with special emphasis on *how to flour your nuts!*"

Him Tarzan

Art Linkletter asked a little girl whom she would choose if she could have two movie stars as parents for a day. Her reply was Art and Zsa Zsa Gabor . . . because Zsa Zsa sounded like an African name, and Art would make a good Tarzan. Art, not thinking, said, "I can't wait to swing from limb to limb. . . . Uh, I mean from tree to tree!"

Off Key

ANNOUNCER: "Excuse me, Senator . . . I am sure that our listening audience would like to hear more about the fine work that your important Congressional committee is doing . . . but unfortunately, Margaret Truman is about to sing."

We Don't Mean United Press

SPOT ANNOUNCEMENT: "This is KLZ-TV, Denver . . . . When you are thirsty, try 7-UP, the refreshing drink in the green bottle with the big 7 on it and *U-P* after!"

Hold That Line

SPORTSCASTER: "Do you find the Chicago Bears have very complicated plays?"
COACH: "I've talked to some defensive players, and they are all pretty simple!"

You're Getting to be a Habit With Me

On the Jack Paar TONIGHT SHOW, Eva Gabor, wanting to tell Paar that she watched his show every night, came out with this classic. "You know, Jack, I go to sleep with you every night!"

This Must be the Place

COMMERCIAL: "This special offer is good for tomorrow only, and the sale will take place at our wholesale whorehouse . . . I beg your pardon . . . the sale will take place at our wholesale warehouse!!!"

Don't Call Me, I'll Call You

This occurred on a television dramatic presentation during the Christmas season. During a scene in which a group of carolers was singing, an actor was supposed to go up to a friend of his who was a member of the group, and greet him warmly with, "George, yah ol' buzzard, ah ain't seen yah in a long time." However, what came out was this, much to the chagrin of all. "George, yah ol' bastard, ah ain't seen yah in a long time." P.S. The actor ain't been around in a long time.

One Track Mind

On the Steve Allen late-night program, Steve interviewed an authority on health:

STEVE ALLEN: "What is your suggestion for a healthy way to start the day?"

GUEST: "First thing in the morning, drink five gallons of water.

STEVE ALLEN: "And then?"

GUEST: "Then you go to the bathroom."

STEVE ALLEN: "What kind of breakfast would you recommend?"

GUEST: "First you go to the bathroom."

STEVE ALLEN: "Please . . . I'm asking about breakfast."

GUEST: "First you go to the bathroom."

STEVE ALLEN: (HYSTERICALLY): "The bathroom . . . the bathroom . . . I mean the breakfast . . . the breakfast!!!"

Ace Is Wild

NEWSCASTER: "Also in attendance was former Governor Joe Foss, famed flying ass of World War II."

On the Button
COMMERCIAL: "So, cold sufferers, stop at your drug store first
thing tomorrow and pick up a bottle of Vicks Naval Spray!"

Junior Announcer

Steve Allen recalls the time when he was an announcer in Phoenix, Arizona, and a fellow announcer introduced a news program in this fashion: "Stay tuned for Fulton Lewis and the Jews . . . I mean Fulton Lewis, Jr., and the news . . . and now Mr. Junior!"

Crack the Whip

TV WANT ADS: ". . . and anyone who qualifies for any of these jobs can phone our station. Today we are looking for someone to fill a spot as an efficient *sadistical* secretary . . . with no bad habits and who is willing to learn."

Sonny Tufts? ? ?

Sonny Tufts, who has been the butt of many a good-natured kidding, was being interviewed on radio. He blooped, "I don't give a goddamn what newspaper people write about me . . . (PAUSE) . . . I'm awfully sorry about my language . . . really, I'm goddamned sorry!"

A Beaut

During the course of the Miss America Pageant choosing the 1968 beauty queen, Bert Park's microphone went dead just as he was to sing the pageant's traditional theme song "There She Goes, Miss America."

A dutiful announcer on a station carrying the network special told viewers: "Bert Parks' singing is not the fault of your local station . . . it's due to network audio problems during the crowing . . . I mean *crowning* of 'Miss America.' As soon as difficulties are restored, we will hear him sing."

Kooks

The following blooper occurred on an evening network news program: "For the latest report on racial strife in the South, we switch you to our reporter in Montgomery, Alabama." "After a night of tension here in Alabama caused by burnings attributed to members of the Ku Ku Lux Kan . . . Klu Klutz Klan . . . the Que Que Klux Klan . . . *(in exasperation) the KKK! . . .*"

Everybody Loves Somebody Sometime

When Dean Martin and Jerry Lewis were teamed together they made a motion picture for Paramount entitled *The Caddy*. They made several spot commercials, plugging the picture. This is how one of the printable takes went: "Hello, everybody, this is Dean Martin." "And this is Jerry Lewis, telling you to see our latest picture for Paramount called *The Caddy*." Dean went on to say, *"The Caddy* is one of the most righteous pictures you will ever see—" Jerry interrupted, "Righteous? Where the fuck do you see 'Righteous?' That's riotous, you greaseball!"

False Impressions

Eva Gabor appeared as a guest on "The Merv Griffin Show." Merv asked if she was afraid of being robbed after appearing on the program with her sparkling necklace being shown on the camera. Merv kept looking at her necklace, which draped her low-cut gown. She replied, "You know, Merv, everything I got is fake. . . . I mean jewelry!"

Fly-By-Night

TV personality Hugh Downs relates the story about movie actor Adolphe Menjou, for years one of America's Ten Best-Dressed Men, who appeared as a guest on the original Jack Paar "Tonight Show." Mr. Menjou, the epitome of fashion, was told by the unpredictable Paar, "Mr. Menjou, you have failed to activate your zipper!"

From Out of the Blue

Guests on an interview show were discussing the 1969 Academy Awards. A film clip from *Butch Cassidy and the Sundance Kid* was shown in which Butch and Sundance jumped over a cliff uttering a four-letter word. One of the interviewees had commented that this objectionable word was censored. Another guest replied, "Yes, they cut the shit out of *Butch Cassidy*."

Small Wonder

Dr. David Reuben, whose sex book has been a best-seller, appeared as a guest on the Johnny Carson "Tonight" program. He tried to make a point by saying that in this space age we can send an astronaut two hundred ninety-three thousand miles, but he can't get within seven inches of his target. Before he could explain his thought, actor Tony Randall, also a guest, chimed in with, "What's this about an undersized astronaut?"

Knots to You

When I appeared with David Frost as his guest on his TV program, he related this blooper which occurred on the BBC in England. An actor in a dramatic moment was supposed to have said, "Truss the victim up in my tie." However, in the excitement of the action he blooped, "Tie the victim up in my truss."

Look Before You Leak

The following occurred on the NBC-TV panel show called "You're Putting Me On." The situation called for comedian Orson Bean to supply clues to comedienne Peggy Cass so that she might guess the unknown word, "leak."

ORSON: "What have you got when you need a plumber?"
PEGGY: "A flood."
ORSON: "From a faucet?"
PEGGY: "A drip."
ORSON (*in exasperation*): "When you gotta go, you gotta
    go."
PEGGY: "A leak."

Dead or Alive

"The Ed Sullivan Show" originally was titled "Toast of the Town." At the end of one of Ed's Sunday night programs, the announcer closing the show told the network of viewers that "Ed Sullivan came to you *alive* from CBS in New York."

Promises, Promises

Sportscaster Al DiRogadus, doing a pregame warm-up before the championship Oakland Raider–Kansas City Chiefs football game blooped the following "Today we are going to see a sensational football dame! GAME!"

Below the Belt

Joe Garagiola, emceeing the audience-participation program "He Said–She Said," quizzed celebrity contestant Hugh Downs. The format called for the celebrity's wife to appear on camera. The questions and answers went like this:

JOE: "What was your first impression of your wife?"
HUGH: "Immoral."
JOE: "How come?"
HUGH: "I was hit on the knee by a golf ball and she said it was a good thing it wasn't any higher. She meant *harder!*"

Fair Game

There is no way a TV football fan can completely ignore a Cleveland player named Fair Hooker. ABC-TV tried, and the commentary team of Keith Jackson, Howard Cosell, and former Dallas Cowboy Don Meredith did their best to play it cool during the course of a New York Jets and Cleveland Browns game. But it was mischievous Don, finally defying all Madison Avenue taboos, who nonchalantly observed, "Isn't Fair Hooker a great name?"

Try Geritol

NEWSCASTER: "In Washington, the Senate is discussing giving funds to aid in reasearch for the new Super-Tonic Transport . . . er Super Sonic Transport!"

Simon Says

DISC JOCKEY: ". . . and now we hear selections from the latest Simon and Garfuckel release. . . . Take it away, Simon and Garfunkel!"

Eeny, Meeny, Miny, Mo

On a man-on-the-street interview program, passers-by were asked their opinions of the various provocative skirt lengths. The interrogator directed his mike at the first female he saw, and this was the result. "I have a street walker over here. (*Apologetically*) I'm sorry, madam. I didn't mean it that way. (*Flustered*) Do you prefer the mindee, meenie, or moxie?"

Honesty Is the Best Policy

On "Let's Make a Deal," popular audience participation program, emcee Monty Hall asked a lady in the "Nondealing" area of the audience the question that he regularly asks the entire audience. "And what happens every Saturday night at seven-thirty." Instead of the usual answer, "Let's Make a Deal," she cracked up the audience with, "I take a bath."

Play Ball!

While watching a Cleveland Indians–Oakland Athletics baseball game, Bob Neal (Cleveland announcer) noticed that owner Charlie O. Finley had come up with another gimmick at his ball park. He had put ball girls along the foul lines instead of ball boys. Mr. Neal blooped, "It appears that Mr. Finley has decided to let girls chase the boys' balls instead of boys chasing boys' . . . *boys' chasing balls!*"

A Nose for News

NEWSCASTER: "Again—Scotch Soup covers the nose."

Wild Announcer
STATION PROMOTION: "See Jack Paar's wildlife on NBC. That is, his wildlife TV special on lions on NBC."

Take Me Out to the Ball Game
During one of the lulls at a Minnesota Twins baseball game, the camera took some close-ups of the fans in the stands. The sportscaster observed two young neckers seated behind third base. He innocently remarked, "Ha, there's two lovers in the stands. He kisses her on the strikes, and she kisses him on the balls."

Hard of Hearing
Heard on "The Newlywed Game," ABC's popular audience-participation program:
EMCEE: "Now, wives, how would you describe your mattress on your honeymoon—soft, medium, or hard?"
WIFE: "Was that before or after we were married?"

Soap in Mouth
SOAP OPERA: "Dad, when Mary told me that she was going to leave me after all these years, and was taking the children with her . . . well, I was just flabberbastard . . . er . . . a faggerbastard . . . *flaggergasted!*"

Order, Please

During a "live" telecast of the KRAFT THEATRE, the dramatic excitement of the most suspenseful moment of the play was reached when above the actors' voices was heard, *"Who ordered the ham on rye?"* The luncheonette delivery boy had walked right into the studio unobserved.

He Floored 'Em

Tex Antoine, who is known for his Uncle Weathbee forecaster character on NBC-TV, accidentally dropped his crayon on the floor while doing his nightly weather forecast. He picked it up and told his listeners that "tomorrow's *floorcast* is for cloudy weather."

Little Boy Lost

An announcer broadcasting a Pittsburgh Pirate baseball game on radio described a pop fly that was hit in the direction of the Pirates' five-foot-five shortstop, Clem Kosherek. As the little infielder disappeared from view behind third base, the sportscaster came out with . . . "Where the hell did Kosherek go?"

Playing in the Cracks

ANNOUNCER: "And now, Van Cliburn playing Tchaikovsky's *Piano Concerto Number One* in Blee Fat Minor . . . I beg your pardon, that should be Fee Blat Minor!!!"

False Start

ANNOUNCER: "Our next selection to be sung by our great baritone soloist is Rachmaninoff's 'Oh, Cease Thy Sinning, Maidenform.' . . . That should be, 'Oh, Cease Thy Sinning, Maiden Fair.' (Off mike) Oh, great, Maidenform is a bra!"

Sir?

LOWELL THOMAS: "This report is credited to the president of the British Broad of Trade, Sir Stifford Crapps. . . . Cripps!"

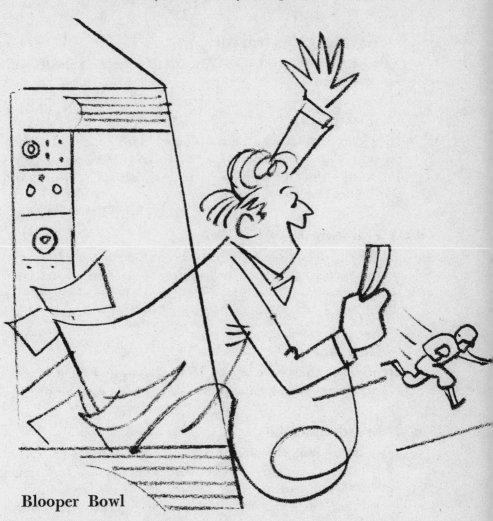

Blooper Bowl

Sportscasters very often get carried away by the excitement of
the moment. Here is a classic example.

"It looks like a pass . . . it's INTERCEPTED on the 30 yard
line . . . he's to the 40, crosses mid-field to the 50 . . . he's
to the 40 . . . he's running wild . . . to the 30, the 20 (hysterically) LOOK AT THAT SONOVABITCH RUN!!!!"

You Can't Win 'em All

STATION PROMOTION: "Hear latest erection results with David Dick on CBS."

Wrong Turn

Dick Cavett was discussing transsexuals with a medical authority on his late night show. Cavett remarked, "You know, doctor, with all of this confusion about which sex is which, you don't know which way to turn."

Praiseworthy

In the dictionary you will find a word spelled P-A-E-A-N and pronounced pe'an. It means to praise. However, an ice-cream sponsor didn't endorse this announcer's choice of words. "And now is a good time to paean Brody's ice cream."

Hey, Man

Sportscaster Curt Gowdy told football fans that "Tim Brown is back deep to receive the punt, while Jerry Logan's uptight."

Broad Statement

Interviewer Phil Donahue had eminent psychologist Harold Greenwald as his guest. Greenwald appeared in connection with his book entitled *The Elegant Prostitute*. Donahue observed that "after visiting with hundreds of prostitutes, Greenwald has come up with a detailed *broad* study of this problem."

Paging Spiro Agnew

Frank Blair, veteran news man on "The Today Show," advised his viewers that NBC will *prevent* TV coverage of the peace demonstrations from Washington.

No Strings Attached

On the TONIGHT SHOW, host Johnny Carson introduced guest star Shari Lewis in this fashion: "And now a girl who is one of the bust pepiteers in the business!!!"

Foot In Mouth

Jinx Falkenberg, the popular female television star, got herself into this amusing tangle.

"I know that I was asked to accept this award for Senator Kefauver as a housewife, because I think that that's what Senator Kefauver did more than anything else—he brought the Senate Crime Investigating Committee into the home, into the kitchen, and gave us all an idea of what was happening in New York City. I know that luckily I was sick the first days of the hearing, so I spent three days in bed enjoying Rudy Halley.

(AUDIENCE LAUGHTER)

"And I must say, I, I, got to know his every move so very well.

(AUDIENCE LAUGHTER)

"No, what I meant . . .

(AUDIENCE LAUGHTER)

"To say is that I missed . . .

(AUDIENCE LAUGHTER)

"I really, you know what I mean."

A Royal Celebration

At the launching of a ship in Norway, a local announcer, with a fine Oxford accent but not too good a grasp of English, was doing the short-wave broadcast when this occurred:

"The Duchess handled the launching beautifully, smashing the champagne bottle against the prow with the aplomb of an expert. The crowd cheered as she majestically slid down the greasy runway into the sea!"

It Was a Great Fight, Ma

Chet Huntley told his viewers during a Gemini live telecast that the Glenn *fight* was witnessed by the largest audience in history.

Dennis the Menace

TELETHON: "This is Dennis James again. I am glad to report that our total has reached a new high. This is due in part to the many *great neckers* at home who have been staying up late watching our program . . . I mean those who live in Great Neck, Long Island!"

Line Forms to the Right

We take you now to Minneapolis to hear the emcee of a program known as POLKA DANCE PARTY.

"Vell, radio audience, dis is a sad day for dis program. Alice Dale, who has been mistress of ceremonies on this show with me, is leafing after fife years. Ve're going to be sorry to see her go. Da producers of dis program and da sponsors have decided that her replacement will come from the ranks of our loyal radio listeners. All you talented young ladies who feel that you can do da job can apply. So ladies, if you want to be my mistress, call Newton 2-0161."

Nutty as a Fruit Cake

Latin bombshell Charo appeared on the Mike Douglas Show. She blooped, "You know, Mike, I nearly got a part in the movie "One Flew Over the Cuckoo's Nuts."

Bodies by Fisher

Ham Fisher, celebrated cartoonist, was a guest judge on the TV beauty contest series to select "Miss New York Television." Ted Steele, popular TV personality, was the emcee, and it was always his custom to conduct a brief interview with the judges. Steele asked Fisher how he liked the girls. Fisher fluffed, "With all the feminine pulchritude around the studio, you have to grasp for breast, I mean gasp for breath."

Out at the Plate

Joe Bolton, WPIX Weatherman, formerly a baseball sports-caster, once lost a job as a result of his excitement during a Newark Bears' ball game, when Ernie Koy hit a home run and Bolton exclaimed, "Jesus Christ! It's over the wall!"

There's a Small Hotel

An emcee on a quiz program asked, "Are there any honey-mooners in the audience?" He got one blushing couple whom he then asked, "Well, what are you doing here, and where are you from?" They answered, "Minnesota." "Are you staying in Los Angeles for a while?" "Yes." "At a hotel?" "Oh, no," replied the bridegroom, "we have relations in the Valley!!!"

A Bad Spell of Weather

WEATHER MAN: "The typhoon that hit China caused devastation everywhere. The mainland has been badly battered in the wake of this disaster. . . . The Chinese people are beginning to dig out with the clearing skies. The weather forecast for that area is for flair and coolie."

People . . . People Who Need People. . . .

DISK JOCKEY: "And now, rock 'n rollers, for the number one record, taking the nation by storm, 'Purple Peter Eaters,' by Sheb Wolley."

Rags to Riches

A young lady on a children's program while relating the story of Cinderella, came up with the following:
"Suddenly Cinderella looked up at the clock—it was striking twelve. . . . As she ran from the palace, she dropped her slipper, but when she reached the door she was again in rags, as the wee-bitching hour struck!"

In the Groove

On smaller radio stations throughout the country, the announcer often doubles as engineer, announcer, producer, director. Let's hear the result of this one man's decision to drop the needle on a transcription, and depart from the studio, for a fifteen-minute break for a cup of coffee. "Remember friends, this is the big holiday weekend coming up, so don't be caught short by unexpected guests. Go to your A and P (NEEDLE STUCK) and P and P and P and P and P. . . ."

Some Yolk

Heard on the Bea Wain–Andre Baruch husband-and-wife radio program.

HUSBAND: "The hen that laid double-yolk eggs will be exhibited at the New York State Fair. However, due to the excessive heat, the hen hasn't laid since last Monday."

WIFE: "This could happen to any of us."

That's the Ticket

In a television dramatic play, an actor portrayed the part of a gangster who had just held up a warehouse. He hurriedly ran to a ticket window in a railroad station to ask the ticket agent for two tickets to Pittsburgh.

"Is this the Allegheny window? Come on, sister, get off the phone. I'm in a hurry, I need two pickets to Tittsburgh!"

Ladies' Home Companion

DISK JOCKEY: "This is Martin Block spinning another record. . . . This time, let's hear from the Mills Brothers, singing 'Be My Wife's Companion'! . . . I beg your pardon . . . that should be, 'Be My Life's Companion.' "

Really Big Star

DISK JOCKEY: "Well, rock 'n rollers, it's time for our mystery-guest contest. If you guess the name of our next artist, our sponsors will send you two tickets to the RKO theatre in your neighborhood. Now the clue to this singer, and this is the only clue I'm going to give you, is that she has two of the *biggest hits* in the country."

Take a Number

DISK JOCKEY: "Before we spin our next Sinatra record, let me tell you about Frank's latest marriage to Mia Farrow. Frank has had three or four wives . . . I'm not sure which one he's on now!"

Many a True Word Is Said In Jest

On I'VE GOT A SECRET, Garry Moore and Wally Cox were putting together some furniture while the blindfolded panel tried to guess what they were doing. In a corner of the studio, a lady was putting together drawers to go in a chest. Time ran out, whereupon Wally Cox commented, "I'm so sorry we didn't get to your drawers." "So am I," replied the lady.

Honesty Is Best Policy

Heard on "Girl Talk" television program, presided over by Virginia Graham: "Once you put down one of her books, you can't pick it up again."

No Holds Barred

NEWSMAN: "And late word from Camp David, President Eisenhower's Maryland retreat, advises that the President and Premier Khrushchev held a private meeting; however, we have no details as to what went on, as newsmen were bored from the conference!"

Party Line

Here is the result of NBC's MONITOR program getting its wires crossed with an announcement of a sermon by Billy Graham.

"Princess Marcella Borghese is visiting MONITOR, to tell us about her life as a Princess and a successful businesswoman. The business angle might not be as romantic as you would imagine, But the princess does (CUT IN) Each Night, In The Open Air, Just Behind The New Multi-Million-Dollar Gymnasium."

Nothing Serious, I Hope

Here's a news item that was handed to a newscaster without being checked in advance.

"In the head-on collision of the two passenger cars, five people were killed in the crash, two seriously."

Medicine Man

Hugh Downs, veteran announcer, was doing a Rem Cough Medicine commercial on the JACK PAAR SHOW. He blooped the following. "So when you have a cough due to a cold, always keep some *Rum* on hand!" He countered with, "This may be good cough medicine, but I don't think it was what the sponsor had in mind."

Alice in Blunderland

Durwood Kirby, on Allen Funt's CANDID CAMERA, came out with this candid blooper. "And now back to Alice Funt!"

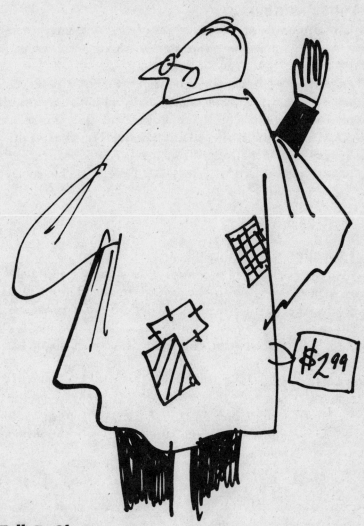

Talk Is Cheap

Heard on radio station CHTM, Manitoba, Canada: The announcer was commenting on the President and stated: "Richard M. Nixon was today sworn in by *Cheap* Justice Earl Warren."

Author, Author

On an audience-participation program, a woman wrestled with the difficult pronounciation of "Alexandre Dumas." She should have left well enough alone.

ANNOUNCER: "Here's your question. There was a famous French author, who wrote many, many famous stories. He is the man who wrote 'The Black Tulip' and 'The Three Musketeers.' What is the name of this famous French author?"

CONTESTANT: "Oh golly . . . I'm nervous . . . let me see . . . OH! Alexandre Dumb-ass! (LAUGHTER) OH! Henry Dumb-ass!"

A Sleeper

Audience-participation programs give sponsors and networks many a headache due to the unexpected and unplanned remarks by the participants, as evidenced by this nationwide broadcast.

EMCEE: "Oh my, sixteen children! Is your husband in the audience?"

CONTESTANT: "Yes."

EMCEE: "Well, let's call him up on the stage. Let's have a nice round of applause for the father of sixteen children. (APPLAUSE) Sir, where did you spend your honeymoon?"

HUSBAND: "Niagara Falls."

EMCEE: "How long were you there?"

HUSBAND: "Eleven days."

EMCEE: "My oh my, you must have seen and done a lot. How did you spend your time?"

HUSBAND: "In bed."

Parlor Game

ANNOUNCERS *"We will return to our LATE SHOW after a brief massage from our sponsor."*

Out of the Mouths of Babes

EMCEE: "How old are you little boy?"

BOY: "Five years old."

EMCEE: "What does your father do?"

BOY: "He works at Tarbide and Tarbon Company (Carbide and Carbon Chemical Company).

EMCEE: "What do they make there?"

BOY: "Light bulbs and toilet paper."

EMCEE: "What makes you think that?"

BOY: "That's what daddy always brings home in his lunch bucket!"

Bringing Up the Rear

On I'VE GOT A SECRET, actress Betsy Palmer took her turn questioning two mayors and two policemen who happened to be standing behind her.

She blooped, "Does your secret have anything to do with the officers behind?"

Inside Joke

When a station was suddenly cut off the air, the announcer, remembering past instances, dutifully switched on the dead mike and said, "Ladies and gentlemen, due to difficulties beyond our control, we are off the air."

Off Course

NEWSCASTER: "And from the latest report it appears that work is progressing rapidly at the famed intercourse canal! . . . That should be, intercoastal canal."

Candid Cameron

CAMEL'S NEWS REEL *had a mix-up due to an AT&T switching error, when John Cameron Swayze said, "And now to Roy Neal in Philadelphia." Roy Neal's voice came on, but the picture was of a Washington correspondent, sitting back in a swivel chair, his heels on a desk, reading a newspaper. Suddenly a voice cut in, "Good grief, we've got Washington!"*

Forks and Spoonerisms

STATION BREAK: "This is WCAR Detroit. Before or after the theatre, be sure to drop in at the Palm Gardens Restaurant for a pretail cockmeal."

Time to Retire

An announcer picked up a script one day and read it on the air, exactly as it was handed to him. It was a Bulova commercial, the standard time signal, with some additions to be made at appropriate times. Here is what the listener heard: "It's 8 P.M. Bulova Watch Time. On Christmas, say Merry Christmas, and on New Year's, say Happy New Year."

He's Got Poisonality

TONY CANZONERI appeared as a panelist on the Rube Goldberg TV show. The program featured cartoon charades, and panelists were supposed to guess sayings, book titles, movie titles, etc., as they were drawn by Goldberg. Tony, arriving late, was given an answer in advance, to keep his average answers respectable. He was told that the correct answer to one of the charades was "poison ivy." Much to the embarrassment of everyone, he answered "poison ivy" to the first question, the answer to which happened to be Henry Wadsworth Longfellow. He raised his hand and answered "poison ivy" to the second cartoon charade. The answer to this was King Philip III. And so on and on for eight questions, he answered "poison ivy!" The ninth cartoon showed a bottle of poison, and ivy growing on the side of a building. Poor Tony figured it was time to stop answering.

Frank-ly Speaking

WHAT'S MY LINE?, the forerunner and brightest of all TV
panel programs, had an anxious moment when Ava Gardner
appeared as a mystery guest. Her identity was supposed to be
guessed by the blindfolded panelists. Her appearance came
at a time when she was having marital difficulties with Frank
Sinatra. The panelists began shooting their usual questions at
the mystery guest, and all was going well until the question
"Are you married?" was asked. Ava said, "Yes." The next question was "Are you glad?" At this point, Stopette, the sponsor,
paid for a full minute of silence.

Blues in the Night

DISK JOCKEY: "To continue on with the music of the NIGHT
TRAIN SHOW, we dig into the past to bring out an old blues
standard, 'I've Got a Crush On You.' And here to sing it,
The Queen of the Booze . . . Miss Dinah Washington!"

Let's Go to the Movies Instead

ANNOUNCER: "Tune in on Monday to find out if Perry Mason
solves this baffling mystery. I'm sorry, on Monday the program
will not be on, due to a special broadcast. Tune in on Tuesday.
I'm sorry, on Tuesday the program is going to be pre-empted
by a speech by Secretary Dulles. Tune in on Wednesday—no,
you'd better consult your papers for the correct time, and
when you find out, please let me know!"

Scoring With the Girl

SPORTSCASTER: *"Montreal hockey fans will be happy to learn
that their star goalie made his first girl in the last few minutes
of play."*

Cut Him Off!

A newscaster was carried away by the excitement of the Cuban invasion. He tried to tell his radio audience about the mobilization of anti-Castro forces.

"Consensus of newsmen's opinions in Havana and Miami is that the people of Cuba are beginning to join antro-Castrate forces . . . anti-Castrate forces!"

Remember the Al and Moe

ANNOUNCER: "You will find Manischewitz wine just right for the holidays, tangy and delicious. This fine wine is also good for any occasion, so remember the Maine, Manischewitz . . . name Manischewitz!"

High Infidelity

MUSIC COMMENTATOR: "Be with us again next Saturday at 10:00 P.M. for the program titled HIGH FIDELITY—a program designed to help music lovers increase their reproduction!"

Hair Bob

Comedian Bob Hope told his radio audience, "Women are wearing bathing suits so short this year that they'll have to get two haircuts."

X Marks the Spot

NEWSCASTER: "Police are now swarming to the scene from all over the county. . . . First reports have it that numerous articles of her clothing were torn and scattered about the scene, and there was evidence of teeth marks on both her . . . (PAUSE) . . . well, that is . . . there were teeth marks on different parts of her body."

Buck Buck Bucket

HILLBILLY DISK JOCKEY: "And now, Zeke Parker sings 'My Hole Has a Bucket In It.' . . . Sorry . . . wrong number . . . that should be, 'My Bucket Has A Hole In It'.—That's quite a difference!"

Sock It To Him!

Sportscaster Chris Schenkel blooped, "The forward pass was caught by a New York Giant receiver . . . with an excellent maneuver he got by a Washington defender . . . he faked him right out of his jocks! . . . (PAUSE) . . . and his shoes as well!"

Hot Off the Griddle

Bill Cullen, master of ceremonies of THE PRICE IS RIGHT, was reading the list of prizes being given away on the program. He said, "And to help you with your cooking, we are giving away an assortment of electrical saucepans, frying pans, etc., and a dutch oven with a *girdle* . . . er, I mean, griddle."

Busman's Holiday

COMMERCIAL: "Remember . . . if you are going a'partying on New Year's Eve, it might be easier and wiser to take the bus than to drive after imbibing. . . . So remember, 'Go by bus and leave the drinking to us!'"

Double Your Pleasure

Johnny Carson, a master of the ad lib, interviewed a couple on his WHO DO YOU TRUST? program.

CARSON: "Do you have any children?"

MAN: "Yes, we have twins, 3½ years old."

CARSON: "That's about the greatest labor-saving device in the world!"

Mental Lapse

NEWSCASTER: "After her apprehension by local authorities, Miss Ellen Benson was confined to a menstrual institution for an indefinite period."

What's Good for the Goose

NEWSCASTER: "Former Vice President Nixon's campaign for Governor of California got a goose today from former President Eisenhower. . . . that should read, got a boost today . . . I'm terribly sorry."

Record on the Bum

ANNOUNCER: "And now we are going to hear a recording of Rimski-Korsakov's 'Bum of the Flightful Bee.'"

Unisex

"Today I would like to explain to all you boys and girls how to go about forming your own 4-H club. The chief requisite is to have an adult leader, like myself, which can be a man or woman or a combination of both."

Queen for a Day

EMCEE: "Well, Mrs. Conklin, you have fifteen seconds in which to answer the question. A correct answer is worth a toaster, a waffle iron, a mixer and an eight-cubic-foot refrigerator. Which woman was known as the Good Queen Bess?"
CONTESTANT: "Bess Truman."

Oh Nurse!

PUBLIC SERVICE ANNOUNCEMENT: "Attention young ladies! Attention young ladies! Your country needs your services. Hospitals throughout the nation are greatly understaffed. Nurses are urgently needed. Volunteer to be one of America's white-clapped ladies of mercy."

Candid Mike

Microphone equipment is becoming smaller and less conspicuous. At a wrestling match, an announcer was busily describing the action in the ring, when he was approached by a wrestling fan.
"It's nice to see we have such a nice crowd here tonight. It's a great turnout; we've got some wonderful matches for you. Now the main event of the evening is gonna be two falls out of three. Chief Bender is going to wrestle with Sando Kovacs—promises to be real exciting. First let's get a word in from our sponsor . . ." (OFF MIKE) "Hey, Mac! Where's the can?"

Lucky Pierre

ANNOUNCER: "It's Music time! Tonight featuring the sounds of Phil Spitoonly . . . Spitalny, and his forty pieces! That is, his all-ghoul orchestra . . . girl orchestra!"

It's What Up Front That Counts

This question was put to the JUVENILE JURY members by moderator Jack Barry: "When you grow up and get married, what would you like your husband or wife to look like?" One five year old said his ideal was Rosemary Clooney, because, he said, "She's got beautiful blue eyes, blonde hair—and a nice body." He added—with gestures—"especially up here . . ."

Cherry Jubilee

KID SHOW: "And for all you kiddies, we are going to dish out cherry ice cream on today's program in celebration of today, February 22nd, George Birthington's Washday!!"

The Cat's Meow

A rock 'n roll disc jockey inadvertently picked up a recording left in his studio by a previous program which featured an hour of concert music. He picked up a recording of a Rachmaninoff concerto and gave it the following introduction. "Now here's a selection that features Rock Maninoff, must be some new cat. Let's give it a listen to."

A New Platform

ANNOUNCER: "This is Station WJSV in Washington, D.C. Pardon me, that's been changed . . . this is Station WTOP in Washington. Stay tuned for PAPLES PLEATFORM which follows over WPOT. That is, PEOPLE'S PLEATFORM."

Stone Face

"Stay stoned for the Rolling Stones . . . next on the 'Ed Sullivan Show'!"

That's My Pop

QUIZ PROGRAM: A young lady contestant on NAME THAT TUNE was asked to name a tune which happened to be "Christopher Columbus." The emcee gave her this hint. "If he didn't do what he did, you wouldn't be here today." Her quick answer was—"My father!!"

Practical Joker

NEWSCASTER: "The minister was covered with papers and rubrish, then drenched with kerosene and set afire. The murderer then set the entire house afire . . . More sports after this message from our sponsor."

Quite a Dish

QUIZ PROGRAM: "Are you ready for your next question? Well, you will be twenty-five dollars richer if you guess the next answer. Remember, if you guess it, our sponsors will send you a twenty-five dollar United States Saving Bond. Now for the question. Russia is famous for its borscht, France is famous for its crepes suzette—now tell me, what famous dish is Hungary noted for?"

ANSWERS "Zsa Zsa Gabor!"

Early Bird

WEATHER FORECASTER: "With the autumn weather now upon us, it seems to be getting early later now!"

Teed Off

"This is Jim Simpson speaking to you from the 18th hole at the National Open. Gardiner Dickenson is getting ready to tee off on this hole, which is 473 years to the green."

Hothead

In the early pioneering days of television's broiling lights, Ted Mack, emcee of the long-running "Amateur Hour," nearly became the victim of a disaster. The stage hands put the hot light close to Ted's head, which made for a well-lighted TV picture, until his hair started to burn!

The Paws that Refreshes

Poor timing and improper pauses can be the source of many a headache for announcers, as evidenced by the improper change of pace.

". . . And the United Nations will adjourn until next week. And now here's a local news item: A lot of villagers were very startled today when a pack of dogs broke loose from a dog catcher's wagon and raced crazily through the fields of a well known tobacco plantation. . . . Friends, does your cigarette taste different lately?"

What's in a Name?

The microphone is a sensitive instrument and can be dangerous. Listen to this female announcer who forgot the mike was listening.

"And now, audience, here is our special TV Matinee guest that we've all been waiting for—world famous author, lecturer and world traveler, a man about town. Mr. er—er, Mr. . . . Oh! What the hell is his name?"

NBC National Biscuit Company

Bill Garden, Director of Special Events at NBC-TV, recalls an announcer who hurriedly finished a religious program to be in time for a station break. He closed by saying, "Cast thy broad upon the waters." He couldn't finish the quotation in time so he concluded with, "This is the National Breadcasting Company."

Stop-Leak-And Listen

"And that's the weather report from the International Airport here at Anchorage, Alaska. Now I'll take a leak out the window to see if it's freezing outside our studio."

Oy Vey!

At a dinner given in honor of President Sadat of Egypt, President Ford introduced him as the President of Israel!

What's Cookin'?

On a cooking show which originated from a Philadelphia station, a housewife told of a delightful new way "to prepare fricken chicasee."

A Day at the Races

In a broadcast originating from Monmouth Race Track in New Jersey, the announcer was making introductory remarks in preparation for the feature race which was to be run in a few minutes. He was running down the entries when he noticed that the horse which was the favorite, named Harass, was not going to run. He reminded the listener to be sure to scratch Harass!

A Pip

MILTON CROSS: "It's the A&P Program, starring Harry Horlick and his A&G Pippsies."

That's Rich

On "Strike it Rich," popular television program produced by Walt Framer, Warren Hull, Master of Ceremonies, interviewed a five year old child whose father was in the United States Army serving in Korea. She wanted to Strike it Rich for an apartment where she would have her own bedroom; whereupon the surprised Hull asked: "With Daddy away in Korea, isn't the apartment you live in with Mommy big enough?" The child's reply was, "During the week I sleep in the bedroom with Mommy, but on the week-ends, when Uncle Charlie comes, they make me sleep on a cot in the kitchen. Anyway, he's not really my uncle."

Bedtime Story

Performers on all-night telethons get very tired. A perfect example is Morey Amsterdam's appearance on one of these marathons for a worthy cause. Here is what came out, at approximately 3 o'clock in the morning. "Mr. and Mrs. Geilgud of the Bronx sent $2.00. And here's another contribution of $2.00 if you will tell Theresa to go to bed." "All right, Theresa will go to bed for $2.00."

I Wonder What's Become of Sally

"Here's an old favorite—Tenor with organ, *Looking for a Girl Named Sally.*"

Scratch Sheet

When Pat Adelman, program director of Station KNOW, Texas, finished preparing the day's schedule, he left it in the control room. Later he made a change—instead of Les Brown's orchestra, he substituted a religious program which was to originate from N. Y. He scratched out Les Brown's and wrote over it, Yom Kippur. When the new announcer came on shift, he picked up the schedule and exhorted his listeners to "Stay tuned for the dance music of Yom Kippur's Orchestra."

Adult Material

EMCEE: "And what do you do for a living, my good lady?"

LADY: "I'm a maid. I do housework, and take care of a large family."

EMCEE: "How large a family?"

LADY: "Well, let's see, there are four boys, three girls, one adult, and one adultress."

Topsy Turvy

On "What's My Line," a program on which occupations are guessed, the contestant was a mattress stuffer. One of the panelists asked this:

"Is your product used by one sex over the other?"

Surprise Party

The following was heard on the "Bride and Groom" radio program.

EMCEE: "And what was the greatest surprise you ever received?"

CONTESTANT: "I got the biggest surprise of my life when my husband came back from the army. I woke up one morning and found him standing by my bed with his discharge in his hands."

Audience roars with laughter.

Quick switch to studio announcer: "There will be a brief pause for organ music."

Tea For Two

"When you're thinking of an all-season thirst quencher, it's a delight—winter or summer—instant White Rose hot or cold Orange Teakoe Pea."

In a Fog

ACTRESS: "The fog was as thick as seepoop."

National Erections

JOHN CHANCELLOR: "Nine Democratic presidential candidates exposed themselves in Washington, D.C., before the Democratic governors."

I've Got a Headache

Carol Wayne, the well-endowed gal who plays the "matinee lady" on The Tonight Show, told Johnny, "Since I've had my baby, I'm almost too tired for you at night."

Handy Andy

On *Exploring The Unknown,* a science program, Andre Baruch, reading a commercial for a large corporation called it "the largest producers in the United States of Magnossium, Alleeminum, and Stool."

A Natural

On *Two for the Money,* popular quiz program sponsored by a cigarette company, Herb Shriner, the Indiana Hoosier, asked a contestant, "Are you a natural born citizen of the United States?" "Oh no," the woman replied, "I was born a Caesarean."

A Run for Your Money

"There's excitement in store on our *Million Dollar Movie* tonight with Ann Sheridan—stay tuned as Phillips Milk of Magnesia brings you *Woman on the Run.*"

Off Her Crocker

COOKING SHOW: *"Ladies, our baking recipe for today features another delicious Betty Crocker cake mix special . . . and we are sure your entire family will enjoy this Betty Baker crock mix delight."*

Front and Center

When I was interviewed on BBC-TV 1 in Bristol, England, my interviewer uttered the following. "Before we continue our chat with American TV producer Kermit Schafer, here is our weather girl, Linda Lee, to tell about her warm front."

Beat the Clock

NARRATOR: ". . . and as his trusty little donkey carried Quixote up the road, he could see the gates of the city ahead. Don Quixote's excitement rose as he contemplated the knightly adventures that awaited him." (*Time running out*) ". . . and there we leave Don Quixote, sitting on his ass, until tomorrow at the same time."

Double Trouble

GANGSTER: "Okay you rat, I've got you covered and now I'm going to drill ya."
(*Complete silence*)
GANGSTER: (*Realizing that the sound effects man has run into trouble*)
"On second thought I'm going to slit your throat."
Two shots—The sound man had located his trouble.

What's Mine Is Mine, What's Yours Is Mine

Senator Austin Warren, in mediating the differences between the Arabs and Israelis at the U.N. came out with this classic. "Now let's all try to settle this problem in a true Christian spirit."

Break the Station

ANNOUNCER: "This is Indiana's first broad-chasing station."

Pocket Pool

A contestant on a quiz program was asked, "What do you find on pool tables that you find in men's trousers?"
The answer should have been pockets.

Good Show

When I appeared as a guest on the Dinah Shore program from Hollywood, fellow guest, British actor Michael York told of some of the fluffs that occurred in England. He told of the classic spoonerism which has trapped many a British announcer. One poor chap told his radio audience that they were listening to the BBC, the British Broadcorping Castration!

Tall Story

QUIZMASTER: "What is the Taj Mahal?"
CONTESTANT: (*After hemming and hawing*) "I'm afraid I don't know."
QUIZMASTER: "I'm awfully sorry, but you should know that the Taj Mahal, located in India, is the greatest erection man has ever had for woman since time immemorial."

Slide, Kelly, Slide

DIZZY DEAN: "The score is tied, and the runners on second and third are taking a lead off their respectable bases. There goes the runner . . . he slud into third base!"

He Blew It

ANNOUNCER: "Yes, there is no doubt that Stephen Foster was one of the greatest, if not the greatest writer of American folk music. His spirituals rank high among the music the world likes best. And now, Stephen Foster's immortal song, 'Old Jack Blow.'"

Strange Interlude

One lesson an announcer learns is to make sure he is off the air before he makes any private comments. But even the greatest sometimes slip. A legend is Uncle Don's remark after he had closed his famous children's program. He thought his mike was cut off the air when he said, "I guess that will hold the little bastards."

12 O'Clock High

Heard on the twelve o'clock news over NBC:
The rumor that President Nixon would veto the bill comes from high White Horse souses.

Just Ducky

COMMENTATOR: "All the world was thrilled with the marriage of the Duck and Doochess of Windsor."

Just Deserts

NEWSCASTER: "Since the G. I. Sergeant James Hermann was refused by the Russians, he has been convicted of desertion, sentenced to three years of hard labor, and been given a desirable discharge."

One of a Kind

Lawrence Welk blew this intro on his syndicated TV show: "We're going to do a medley of songs from World War Eye!"

Crazy man, Crazy

Let's listen to an introduction of famous news commentator, John Cameron Swayze.
"Stay tuned to John Solomon Cwayze and the news!"

Boomerang

PLAY-BY-PLAY ANNOUNCER: "Here comes the pitch—it's a well-hit ball, going toward straightaway center field . . . going . . . going . . . and it's curving foul!"

Jam Session

While doing research for my television specials, titled "Kermit Schafer's Blunderful World of Bloopers," I came across a Betty Furness Westinghouse refrigerator commercial which occurred on a weekly TV program that I produced on NBC-TV. This was the moment when the refrigerator door got stuck.

When she couldn't get it open on the first two tries, she gritted her teeth and said, "Who's the comedian?" The camera came in close until her face filled the entire screen while she continued the commercial, albeit falteringly. Meantime, the shadows of hands could be seen frantically working on the refrigerator until the camera pulled back showing a doorless, hingeless refrigerator!

Shake Down, I Mean Count Down

NEWSCASTER: "The area around Cape Canaveral has certainly grown in leaps and bounds, largely due to the influx of Army racketeers and their families."

Rumble Seat

Various station cut-ins play havoc with programs heavily laden with commercials, as per this example. "Our lovely model, Susan Dalrymple, is wearing a lovely two-piece ensemble. . . . (STATION CUT-IN) . . . with a rear engine in the back!"

Sam, You Made the Pants Too Long

COMMERCIAL: "Ladies, you will enjoy Sam's department store shopping, which features clothing for the entire family. Our special this week is men's trousers . . . so for the biggest thing in men's trousers . . . come in and see Sam!"

Boy Oh Boy!

On KMOX, St. Louis, during an interview with the assistant manager of Holiday Inn at Collinsville, Illinois, they were talking about the chess tournament held at the Holiday Inn. There was this five-year-old kid that was beating everyone. The announcer asked the assistant manager if he was going to challenge the kid. He replied, "There is no way a five-year-old kid is going to make an asshole out of a 61-year-old man."

At a Loss for the Right Words

COMMERCIAL: "So remember folks, we have all the latest models in hard tops and convertibles at prices you can't afford to miss. Yes folks, at Courtesy Motors your loss is our gain."

Don't Miss It!

STATION BREAK: "Be sure not to miss THE COMING OF CHRIST, Wednesday, 8:30 P.M., 7:30 Central Time."

Blankety Blank

DISK JOCKEY: "Our all-request recorded program continues with a request from Elmer Peters, who phoned in to please play for my wife who just had a baby at St. Luke's Hospital. . . . 'I DIDN'T KNOW THE GUN WAS LOADED'!!"

I Hear You Calling Massa

MUSICIAN: "For my next selection, I would like to play a medley of Old Stephen Foster favorites; among them will be 'Jeannie with the Light Brown Hair,' 'My Old Kentucky Home,' and 'My Ass Is In The Cold, Cold Ground.' "

Do Not Play with Matches

On a TV Science program, a professor of Physics was experimenting with a gas. At the conclusion of his program, he came up with this classic. "I see our time is running out, and to be on the safe side and before I do anything else, I'll have to ask you to bear with me for a moment while I get rid of my gas!"

Cheese and Crackers!

COMMERCIAL: "Men, when you take your favorite girl out for dinner, atmosphere means an awful lot. You will find the best German food and the best sauerbraten at Joe's Rat Celler . . . er . . . Rathskeller."

Pots and Pans

ANNOUNCER: "We will now hear chamber music from the Potts ensemble!"

Judy, Judy, Judy

DISK JOCKEY: "And now here's an ever-popular favorite, July Garland singing, 'Ding, Ding, Ding Went the Trollop.' "

I Wish I Were Single Again

LOCAL NEWS: "Mr. Baker, who applied for the job, seemed to be very well qualified. He is obviously a man of sound judgment and intelligence. Mr. Baker is not married."

State of the Union

NEWSCASTER: "Judge Walter Thompson warned the manufacturers that the courts had already handed down the decision, and he would look with disfavor upon anyone who tampered with his union suit."

I Ain't Got No Body

SPORTSCASTER: "DiMaggio is back, back, back to the wall, his head hits it, it drops to the ground, he picks it up and throws it to third."

Charge! ! !

COMMERCIAL: "Come in at the sign of the clock, where it only takes six months to open a three-minute charge account!"

All Balled Up

DISC JOCKEY: "And that was 'South Town' sung by the Blue Bellies . . . I mean, the Blue Balls . . . the Blue Belles!!"

One-Way Passage

Let's listen to this proud professor of music telling the radio audience about one of his pupils, on a program that originated from a well-known college of music.

"Our next number is Tchaikovsky's violin concerto, featuring our own violin virtuoso, Sol Tannenbaum. You will notice that Mr. Tannenbaum plays passages of ease with the greatest of difficulty."

Figures Do Not Lie

NEWSCASTER: "Our annual report of the committee reveals that health conditions aren't all they should be. The city's beaches have an appalling amount of litter, and a check at the municipal swimming pools reveals some startling figures!"

Stoned

LOCAL NEWS: "And from Mrs. Peyton, President of the Garden Study Club, comes word of a meeting next Friday, There will be a lecture by Eleanor Dayton. The topic of her lecture will be 'My Potted Friends!' "

Little Caesar

On the Texaco Star Theatre, one of the principal actors played a prominent part in the dramatization of Julius Caesar. He had a very important line whereby he was to introduce Bruce Cabot, who was the star of the Shakespearean play. Here is how the introduction came off. "Hail the conquering hero, great leader of armies, renowned figure in history, Sid Caesar!"

Dangerous Curves

SAFETY PROGRAM: "What would you say is the most dangerous room in the house? You would think either the bathroom or the kitchen. Well, here's a surprise. According to a recent study, one fourth of all accidents take place in the bedroom!"

Whoopee!

FASHION COMMENTATOR: "And now for the latest from the fashion world. It is good news for men. Women are not going to wear their dresses any longer . . . this year."

Don't Forget the Sandwiches

SPORTSCASTER: "The broad jump was won by Harry Crawford of Rice University. Pole vault was won by Dick Staley of S.M.U.; the relay race was won by Texas Christian University. And now the event you've all been waiting for, the thousand-mile dash!"

Peek-a-Boo Boo

DISC JOCKEY: "I think the temperature is dropping. While this record is playing I'll go take a leak at the thermometer."

Killjoy

COMMERCIAL: "At Gimbels for today only, we are featuring a special on fun-resistant panties . . . I do not mean fun-resistant . . . I mean run-resistant!"

Bono No No

Cher Bono was singing "Gypsies, Tramps and Thieves."
At the end of the song the disk jockey announced. "That
was Cher Porno . . . er . . . singing 'Typsies, Gramps and
Thieves . . .' "

Really Convenient

"You will find many attractive features at a Holiday Inn
in your area. Holiday Inns are equipped to perform many
functions, so when you are thinking of having your next
affair, remember a Holiday Inn motel!"

Stop the Music

DISC JOCKEY: "We will continue with our program of un-
interrupted music after this message from our sponsor."

Some Choke

PUBLIC SERVICE ANNOUNCEMENT: "So be sure and visit our
mobile unit where you can get emphysema free for the
asking."

Sleepy Time Gal

Heard on "Secret Storm": "I stayed awake last night dream-
ing about you."

Some Kind of a Nut

COMMERCIAL: "At Wortman's Furniture store, their interior
decorator will give you ideas for your home in every type of
wood. Come in today and see their showroom and be their
guest in their *walled nut room!*"

Honest Abe
COMMERCIAL: "So ladies . : . be sure not to miss our Washington's Birthday special sale on Monday, Lincoln's birthday."

You Can't Tell the Players Without A Score Card

Viewers were watching the exciting Western film titled *Broken Arrows,* which was being presented on "Monday Night at the Movies." A typical scene was being shown where the good guys were huddled around a burning covered wagon shooting frantically at the encircling Apaches, who were getting knocked off with great precision. At this point, superimposed over the action, the following latest football score was shown: "Cowboys 36——Indians 6."

Crop That Out

Heard on station KGO, San Francisco: "And it has been announced that the presidential party will be served the choicest of this year's Lamb *Crap.*"

Jim Dandy

NEWSCASTER: "James Hoffa was scheduled to address prisoners of his Teamsters Union . . . *pensioners!*"

Can the Announcer

"This portion of 'Petticoat Junction' is brought to you by the American Home Company, makers of fine products for your can . . . I mean American *Can* Company . . . makers of fine products for your *home!*"

An American In Paris

"Stay tuned to NBC for developments as the American delegation seeks a peace . . . . spelled p-e-a-c-e . . . . in Paris."

Vive la France

On Red Benson's TV Show, NAME THAT TUNE, two contestants, a beautiful French girl and a sailor, were trying for the prize. The orchestra played "The Anniversary Waltz." The beauty said, " 'Oh, How Ve Danced on Ze Nite Ve Vere Ved.' " "No," replied Red, "that's a line from it." Then turning to the sailor he said, "If you were married to this beautiful girl tonight, what would you be singing a year from now?" The sailor replied: " 'Rock-a-bye-Baby!' "

To Err Is Human

EMCEE: "I don't understand . . . a moment ago, you said you had two children . . . now, young lady, you tell me you are not married?"
YOUNG LADY: "Can't a girl make a mistake once in a while?"

Up, Up and Away

On the New York broadcast of the Mike Douglas show, a woman asked Chad Everett what his measurements were. His reply was "Which one?" Later on, another woman asked Everett when he enjoyed his first sexual encounter. CBS bleeped his answer. However, a lip reader wrote that his answer was "As soon as I was able to get it up!"

STATION

BREAK

WE WILL RETURN TO
KERMIT SCHAFER'S BLUNDERFUL WORLD
OF BLOOPERS
AFTER WE PAUSE TO MEET
THE TV BLOOPER CALENDAR GIRLS

Bosom Pals

JIMMY DEAN: "This gal has two big things going for her!"

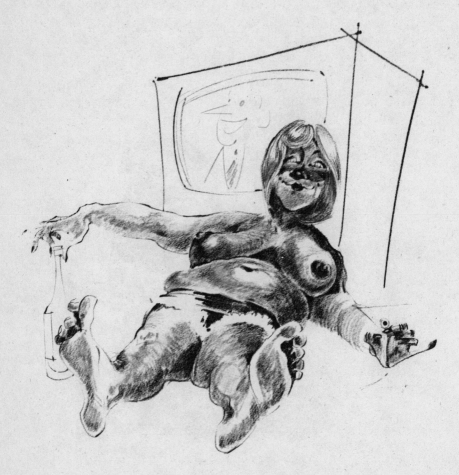

Broad Smile

STATION BREAK: "Stay stewed for the nudes!"

The Old Pro

COMMERCIAL: "Ladies, our shoe stores are featuring
sneakers that are ideal for street walking!"

Pin Up Girl

"Stay tuned for your community bulletin broad!"

All Screwed Up

CONTESTANT: "I'm a housewife and I have thirteen children . . . My husband operates an automatic screwing machine!!"

Farmer's Daughter

"Final results of the FFA contest are: Apple picking won by
Dick Jones. Tractor driving award to Jack Davis. One of our
own girls, Miss Betty Smith, was chosen as the best hoer."

Fore Play

"We now present the winner of the golf event held on four separate golf courses . . . Miss Helen Douglas, our new state intercourse champ!"

Foul Play

COMMERCIAL: "Friday night is poultry night . . . remember, all ladies present will receive a free goose!!"

Great Expectations

STATION BREAK: "Stay tuned for Dickens' immortal classic, Sale of Two Titties . . . er TALE OF TWO CITIES!!!"

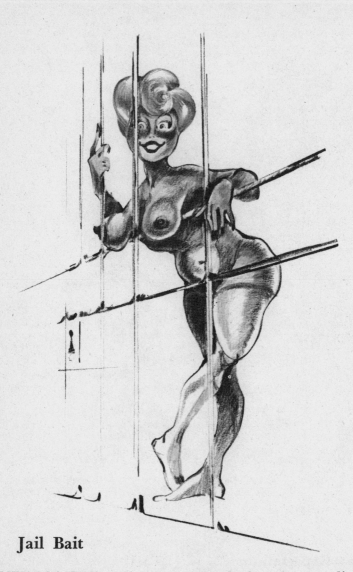

Jail Bait

NEWSCASTER: "She was arrested after she was discovered running through the streets of town in the nude. Police held her several days for observation!"

Small Wonder

ANNOUNCER: "And Dad will love the delicious flavor too . . . So remember it's Wonder Bread for the breast in bed."

A Figure of Speech

COMMERCIAL: "Ladies, now you can have a bikini for a ridiculous figure!"

Ass Backwards

ANNOUNCER: "This portion of Wednesday Night At The Movies was brought to you by Bayer Aspirin . . . and now back to Ava Gardner as the Bare Ass Contessa . . . I mean THE BARE FOOT CONTESSA!!!"

And now back to

BLUNDERFUL WORLD OF BLOOPERS

Love Thy Neighbor

On "The Neighbors" Show, after a heated discussion between a female contestant and her male neighbor, he said, "You are giving me tit for tat. You're getting your tat now, but after the show I'll get my tit!"

Very Disastrous

During the American Forces Network's salute to Veterans Day, the station planned one minute inserts praising ex-soldiers for their patriotism and sacrifices in serving their country. What was heard on the air were one minute preachments to soldiers overseas on how to avoid venereal disease! It seems that the technicians had run the wrong tape cartridges, because on the program sheet, the Veterans Day announcements were written as "V.D. Inserts."

College Try

During the Sugar Bowl game between Alabama and Penn State, Bud Wilkenson blooped, "Joe Paternity . . . Paterno's fine defensive line from Pencil State University . . . er . . . I mean Penn State University has played well."

Tennis Anyone?

On WMAQ-TV this past fall a sports announcer was finishing up his report with this story. "Tennis star Ericka _____ has undergone a sex-change operation and is now known as Eric. So that wraps it up . . . Now on to Jane Pauley who has a story on musical instruments . . ."

Jane: "Yes, and after a word from our sponsor, I'll tell you about the refurbishing of an old organ . . ."

Bright Remark

Sportscaster Curt Gowdy blooped his way through this one: "The Baltimore Colts are a bright young team, and it seems as if they have their future ahead of them."

Cutting Remark

Adlai Stevenson, one of America's great statesmen, was known for his remarkable vocabulary. However, even one as great as he was can fall victim to a prize Blooper. The following occurred during a speech that was broadcast nation-wide: "Protest demonstrations have taken place by workers whose trade union rights have been betrayed, by Catholics whose freedom of expression has been circumcized . . . circumscribed." (AUDIENCE LAUGHTER) He then tried to recover with, "Well, I believe it at least is a Christian right."

Air Time

DISK JOCKEY: "And now some lovely songs from Josh Logan's 'Fanny' "

For the Man Who Has Everything

One of the prizes on the show, "Gambit," was a riding power mower with optional grass catcher. However, the announcer informed the audience that it was "a beautiful riding mower with optional ass scratcher."

Fed Up
Hugh Downs, doing an Alpo dog food commercial on the Today Show, was frustrated by a St. Bernard who was supposed to eat the food with relish during a live commercial. All the dog did, however, was sniff at the bowl and pant into the mike. The exasperated Downs pleaded, "Would you mind explaining why you won't eat?"

For Better or Worse
SPORTSCASTER: Jack Kachave, with a bad knee, limps back to the huddle. He wants to play this game in the worst way . . . and that's exactly what he is doing!

Paging Miss Keeler
The following was heard on the BBC: "I cannot speak for other women, but I have always found that Prime Minister MacMillan satisfied me personally . . . that is, more than any other Cabinet member."

Booze Is the Only Answer
NEWSCASTER: The committee for the charity bazaar starting next Sunday at the Methodist Church has assured us that there will be plenty of booze selling . . . I don't mean booze . . . I mean that there will be plenty of booths selling.

Sing, You Sinners
ANNOUNCER: Our midnight movie tonight features Gene Kelly, Donald O'Connor and Debbie Reynolds in the tuneful 'Sinnin In The Rain' . . . er . . . 'Singing In The Rain.'

Fibber McGee
Newsman Frank McGee, sitting in on The Today Show on NBC-TV, told of ". . . heavy clouds in the wethermost . . . *westernmost* portions and heavy snurf . . . *surf* . . . along the coast!"

He Doesn't Give a Hoot

One night Johnny Carson had an animal trainer as a guest on his Tonight Show. When they had to break for a commercial, Carson advised listeners to: "stay tuned, because right after this we're going to be seeing a horny owl."

Death Takes a Holiday
An announcer at KERV, Kerrville, Texas, read this unnerving bit of information on his "obituary column of the air":

"Karl Smith, 83, a lifetime resident of this city, passed away at his home Tuesday night. Funeral services for Mr. Smith will be held in the chapel of the First Methodist Church. Entertainment will follow in the cemetery. Excuse me, that should have been *interment*."

It's About Time
The early-morning newscaster was apparently not quite awake yet, but he sure woke his listeners up with this agricultural news:

"The farmers in the Annapolis Valley are pleased to announce that this year there will be an abundance of apples. This is particularly good news, because most of the farmers haven't had a good crap in years."

I'd Rather Fight Than Switch
Heard on a Michigan TV station: "Stay tuned for tonight's movie, 'Take the High Ground,' starring Richard Widmark. This is the story of a tough marine sergeant who takes a platoon of fighting men and turns them into a bunch of raw recruits."

Animal Crackers
When Mike Douglas was interviewing Wayne Newton's Japanese wife, they talked about Wayne's love of animals. Mike asked Mrs. Newton, "Have you always liked animals?" "No, not until I met Wayne."

On the Carpet

A KEWI announcer, doing a commercial during the play-by-play coverage of a baseball game, looked up and saw that a batter was at the plate and the next inning was about to start. As a result, he hurried through the end of the commercial, and it came out like this: "If you buy your wall-to-wall carpeting at Ed Marling's this week, Marlings *crapet fartsmen* will install it absolutely free."

Who's On First

During a press conference Senator J. William Fulbright gave the following memorable answer to a reporter's question: "As I said already, they have conducted themselves in the last two or three years, much more discri . . . er, discree . . . discri . . . uh, with greater prudence and discretion than we have, because it is, uh, I . . . I've forgotten what the question was."

Forget Me Not

Heard on WIOD in Miami, Florida: "This is Alan Courtney speaking. Don't forget, tonight at nine, our special guest . . . (PAUSE) . . . will be . . . I forgot."

Give him the Bird

Telephone talk shows on radio are particularly good sources of Bloopers. When Art Merrill was conducting his regular telephone interview program one night on WIOD, Miami, his guest was a representative from Women's Lib. A man called in, and the following conversation ensued:

MAN: Do you realize that all nature is set up in pecking orders?

WOMAN: Yes, and I know that in many animals, the female is at the top of the pecking order.

MAN: But it's a minority.

MERRILL: (interrupting) All right, then what you're saying is that, according to you, in all nature, the man is the pecker and the woman is the peckee.

Cutie Pie
The following was heard on KUTY, Palmdale, California. "On the local news scene the shitty sherriff, I mean the city sheriff, was kept busy with three buglers last night . . . burglars!"

Even Steven
On a particularly lively edition of the NBC-TV Today Show, Edmund Muskie repeatedly referred to host Bill Monroe as "Frank McGee." Listeners were doubly confused when Mr. Monroe began calling Muskie "Senator McGovern."

An Ill Wind
This poor weathercaster made the following remarks about hurricane Agnes: "And as you already know, Agnes really blew the whole city this afternoon."

Peter Piper Picked a Peck of . . .
I wonder what kind of response the local law enforcement people got when a radio station public service announcer read that the police department was in need of "parking peter maids."

Change of Announcer
Overheard on a local television station break: "We'll be right back, after this menopause . . . minute pause!!"

A Beaut
Sometimes a single incorrect letter in a news story can change the entire meaning of a sentence. A copywriter in the midwest was out of a job after giving the newscaster an item which read as follows:

ANNOUNCER: . . . meanwhile, in Rome, a large number of Catholics are petitioning to have the late Pope beautified . . . uh, I believe that should be "beatified."

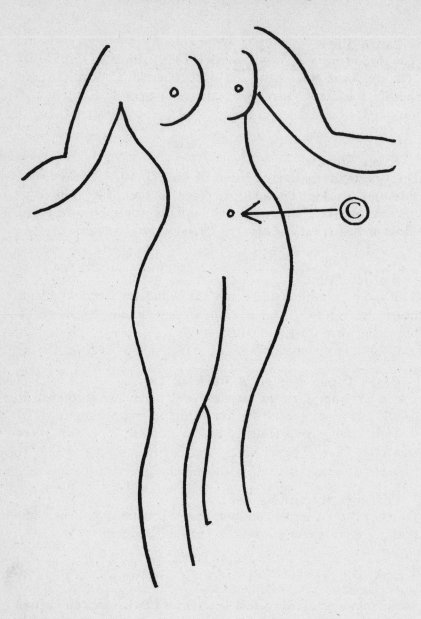

Novel Idea
LOUELLA PARSONS: It is rumored here in Hollywood that
the film company bought the rights to a new navel for Audrey
Hepburn.

No Place Like Home

Heard on "The Edge Of Night": An actor, having just been discharged from the hospital, where he had spent several months lying on his back with a serious illness, looks around the family surroundings and happily exclaims to his wife, "Mary, oh it's so good to be homo . . . (gulp) . . . home."

A Pair of Cities

A well-known Hollywood movie gossip commenator came out with this gem of a Blooper: ". . . and from Rome comes word of a new movie scheduled to go into production soon, starring Sophia Loren. Several locations for the film are being considered for Miss Loren . . . among them Florence and Nipples, Italy . . . er . . . Naples."

Ace in the Hole

"And we disc jockeys have made a special plaque which will go to any golfer who notifies us when he has scoled a hore in one!"

Charity Begins at Home

The following was heard on "The Joey Bishop Show." Joey was telling a socialite guest that he remembered that she was the sponsor of a charity event. Joe innocently asked, "By the way, how was your affair . . . er . . . I mean, tell us about your latest affair."

Jack Be Nimble

Jack Paar appeared in an NBC-TV special entitled "Jack Paar's Diary." Jack had just surfaced from a car submerged in about fifteen feet of water. He was taking a lesson on surviving if his car fell in. He surfaced and started telling about it. Scheduled next was a cut to a commercial, but apparently they stayed on him too long. A few seconds before the commercial, Paar said, "Let's get the hell out of here!"

Communication Gap

Mayor Daley of Chicago was being interviewed on television following the riots during the Democratic convention. The mayor stated "The police in Chicago are not here to create disorder, they are here to preserve it."

Something to Celebrate

During the course of a television documentary, the following was heard: "The Lord Mayor's Show, which celebrates the erection of the new Lord Mayor of London, takes place annually in November . . . that should read *election.*

Ho, Ho, Ho

Station Promotion: "Tonight, it's Bing Crosby and Carol Burnett. See the Christmas special starring Bing and Carol, together again for the first time . . . (OFF MIKE) . . . Hey, who wrote this promo?"

Try a Deodorant

Mike Douglas very often brings on a surprise guest unbeknownst to his co-host. In this instance, the co-host was popular singer-comedienne Pearl Bailey. The surprise guest turned out to be Louis "Satchmo" Armstrong, a very dear and old friend of Pearl's. Mike, probably influenced by Louis's traditional and constant mopping of his brow with his handkerchief, asked Armstrong, "What advice would you give young perspiring performers?"

The Long and Short of It

SPORTSCASTER: Here we are on the fifteenth green where Billy Casper is getting ready to putt . . . Billy, usually an excellent putter, seems to be having difficulty with his long putts. However, he has no trouble dropping his shorts.

Must Be a Convention
SPORTSCASTER: Today's professional football schedule has the Buffalo Bills at Denver, the Oakland Raiders at Denver and the Miami Dolphins at Denver . . . (OFF MIKE) . . . that sounds like a helluva lotta teams at Denver on one Sunday afternoon . . . where in the hell did we get this schedule?

Gigged
Dick Cavett wanted to tell about his guests for that night's show, when he came up with this Blooper: "Hi, I'm Dick Cavett, and tonight my guest is Academy Award Wimmer . . . Academy Award Wimmer . . . there . . . I've done it again . . . Academy Award Winer, Gig Young!"

Let's Be Buddies
President Nixon, on the campaign trail to win support for Republicans running for office in many states, arrived in Miami Beach, where he spoke to a huge throng on behalf of the candidate for the United States Senate, Bill Cramer. He raised the candidate's hand and told voters, "So be sure when election time rolls around next Tuesday, to vote for my old friend . . . er . . . Congressman Bull Craner!"

Screwy Commercial
Movie commercial: "So for a holiday treat you can take the entire family to see . . . this is one picture you will not want to miss. All of the nation's critics love Screws . . . I beg your pardon, that should be Scrooge."

Heads Up
DISC JOCKEY: And now, the hit song from Butch Cassidy and the Sundance Kid, starring Paul Newman, Bert Bacharach's beautiful ballad, "Rain Drops Keep Falling on My Bed!"

Paging Raquel Welch

Heard on the "Outdoor Life" Program: "Our first guest this afternoon is one of the nation's outstanding experts on birds, who has just returned from an extended trip to Australia. In addition to bringing back several parrots, she boasts of owning the largest parateets in captivity."

Nice Trick If You Can Do It
Heard on "The French Chef": "Then you add two forkfuls of cooking oil . . ."

Boy Wonder
During the course of an exciting Oakland Raiders-Kansas City Chiefs football game, sportscaster Curt Gowdy blooped, "The seventy-eight yard drive was led by fourteen-year-old veteran, Lenny Dawson!"

Surprise Party
NEWSCASTER: . . . and from Washington comes word that President and Mrs. Lincoln will spend Nixon's birthday at Key Biscayne, Florida, on February twelfth.

Flipp-Her
Popular TV and recording star, Glenn Campbell, was sitting on the edge of a small concrete fish pond, singing a duet with a female guest. At the end of the number, Glenn spread his arms out in a big finish. His singing companion went flying backwards, falling into the pond for an unexpected bath.

Game Called Because of Wetness
SPORTSCASTER: It's raining again, and it appears just a matter of minutes before play will be called because of the weather. As the Pittsburgh Pirates' pitcher stands on the mound, you can barely see the P.P. on his muddy uniform.

One Up
On the Tonight Show, Johnny Carson was telling how he disliked cabs and had walked to work that evening rather than take a taxi. He told viewers, "A cabbie drove by giving me a peace sign . . . half of which I returned."

A Knockout!

In March of 1969, heavyweight boxer Jerry Quarry won an important nationally-televised bout in Madison Square Garden. A station in Binghamton, New York, infuriated boxing fans by putting commercials between every round, in such a way as to cut off the last few seconds of one round and the first few seconds of the next. All the commercials were for a local sponsor . . . a Ford automobile agency. Imagine the whoops of delight when Quarry, interviewed by ringside commentator, Don Dunphy, stated that for winning the bout, he was receiving a new Pontiac from an Oakland, California dealer!

Hole in One

A disc jockey on KCBQ, San Diego was asking his listeners to call in and try to win a record album. He surprised the radio audience with the following: "All right, stick your finger in the operator's hole and . . . uh, the telephone hole marked operator, that is, and call in now."

Inflammatory Remark

On Channel 32, in Chicago, the evening announcer finished up a commercial for an arthritis relief ointment with this live closing . . . "For more inflammation read the label."

Car Sickness

NEWSCASTER: (READING HEADLINES) ". . . accident on freeway involves four cars, hospitalizes one . . ."

My Old Kentucky Home

WEATHERMAN: . . . and there is a high pressure system around Lexintuck, Kentuky . . . I mean Lexington, Kentuxy . . . you know what I mean.

Chief Red in the Face
A BBC newsreader saved the day and probably his job when he caught himself just in time when reading the following news item about the Chief Constable of Kent: "It has been learned that the Chief Kenstable of . . . and now we turn to news in the world of sports."

Three's a Crowd
In a television interview several years ago, Senator Margaret Chase Smith of Maine was questioned about her presidential aspirations. Asked what she would do if she woke up one morning and found herself in the White House, she replied, "I would go straight downstairs and apologize to Mrs. Eisenhower, and then I would go right home."

Tinkle, Tinkle, Little Star
Pianist Roger Williams appeared on the Mike Douglas Show with Robert L. Green, fashion director for *Playboy* magazine. Green told Williams, "Although I have never met you, I've heard you tinkling many times." Williams came back with, "I've been tinkling since I was a little child."

Oh Mummy!
NEWSCASTER: Enthusiasts from far and wide journeyed hundreds of miles to queue up in some instances for more than six hours outside the British Museum to get a look at King Tutankhamun, the famous mammy.

Do You Still Beat Your Wife?
On the Perry Mason program, Walter Pidgeon, substituting for Raymond Burr, addressed the witness in the following manner: "Answer this question with a simple yes or no . . . what were your feelings toward the murdered man?"

Cool, Man, Cool

Commercial: "This king-size refrigerator is large enough to seat all the nudes of your family . . . suit all the needs of your family!!!"

TV Daddy

Mike Douglas often becomes victim to spoonerisms, unintended interchanges of syllables. One such lapse occurred when he had Milton Berle as his guest. Mike was seriously relating many of Milton's valuable contributions to television, when he said, "Milton, we owe you a gret of dadditude."

'Nuff Said

Heard on ABC-TV's Newlywed Game: "What one thing have you mastered since you have been married?" "Sex."

Aloha

Sportscaster Chris Schenkel was broadcasting the football game between the college all-stars in the annual Hula Bowl game, which was played in Hawaii and beamed to fans nationwide by satellite. Also part of the broadcast team was former Oklahoma football coach Bud Wilkerson and All-American football great O. J. Simpson. A TV camera switched to a pretty coed in the stands, which prompted Schenkel to ask, "Bud, isn't that the young lady who gave us a lei before the game?"

Help!

Barbara Walters, one of the co-emcees on the NBC "Today" show, had talented actress Mercedes McCambridge as her guest. Miss McCambridge was to tell of her gallant victory over alcohol. The well-meaning and usually reliable Barbara told her viewers that her guest was at one time "in dire need of trouble."

Hands Off

Heard on a Smothers Brothers summer show. Just before a commercial break, the announcer blurted out, "Don't play with your knob . . . we'll be right back!"

I'm Not Thirsty

TV personality David Frost was discussing the problems of pollution on his syndicated TV program. He told how important he thought it was for pollution inspectors to "personally pass drinking water."

Out of This World

Heard on "Star Trek," popular science fiction series, when Captain Kirk, the hero, fell in love with a woman who was plotting to destroy a planet: "Millions of people who have never died before will be killed."

Ball Carriers

SPORTSCASTER: The half-back takes a pitchout and is immediately hit behind the line of scrimmage by a crunching, vicious tackle . . . it's a fumble and there are a couple of loose balls on the field.

Slips Don't Count

The emcee on "The Newlywed Game" asked the husbands what size bed they had in the bridal suite on their honeymoon. One of the new grooms confidently blurted out, "A double bed . . . and I know I'm right because we were so used to a king-size bed" . . . which made the bride hide her face during the rest of the program.

Can't Tell Players Without a Scorecard

NEWSCASTER: Also present at the rally were Governor and Mrs. Governor Ronald Reagan . . . that is, Mrs. Governor and Mr. Reagan . . . (exasperated) . . . California's first lady and his wife . . . oh, well . . . I'm sure you know who I mean!

Ball Breaker

A BBC radio announcer apparently had too much holiday spirit, with the following result . . . "We now hear Deck Your Balls With Halls of Helly . . . Deck Your Bells With Balls of Holly . . . er . . . a Christmas selection."

A Lot of Bull

NEWSCASTER: It is the opinion of many observers, that in handling the situation, the President hit the bull's eye on the nose.

When You Gotta Go——

Arlene Francis, popular femcee and panelist on What's My Line, was doing a studio audience warm-up on radio many years ago. She miscalculated the allotted time and said: "There are thirty seconds to go, if anyone has to." This advice was heard by millions of her listeners."

Nuts to You

In his anxiety to please his new sponsor, Chock Full of Nuts, on NBC-TV, popular comedian, Morey Amsterdam, tripped over the client's name and spurted out, "You will enjoy a Jock Full of Nuts Special at lunchtime."

Gentle on My Mind

Station promo: "This Sunday, see the adventures of an Everglades family and a bear, on Gentile Ben . . . that, of course, should be Gentle Ben."

Half Time

Station break: "We will return to the third half of the Virginian in a moment."

C'm up and See me Sometime!

Wild, Wild West

On the "Merv Griffin Show," Arch Obler was talking about the time he had written an Adam and Eve sketch which was to star Mae West. Obler was talking about Miss West's unusual method of making transactions, writing checks and doing business, when he blooped: "I said that because Mae West does all her business in her bedroom. I mean she does everything in her bedroom . . . Now I'm getting in deeper!"

For the Birds
ANNOUNCER: At 8 P.M. we will present another in the series of classic dramatizations as part of this month's Shakespearian festival. Tonight's presentation is Macbeth, considered by many to be the greatest work of the Bird of Avon.

Chorus Persons
NEWSCASTER: The C-47, carrying a planeload of chorus girls bound for a USO destination to entertain troops, was forced down in a jungle somewhere in Africa . . . However, all parsons abroad were reported safe."

I've Got a Secret
Art Linkletter has learned that children don't have many secrets. Just to make conversation, he recently asked a little girl what her mother had told her not to do that day. "She told me not to announce that she was pregnant."

Just Ducky
NEWSCASTER: . . . and Florida's candidate for governor, Reuben Askew, accused incumbent Governor Claude Cluck . . . er Kirk of ducking the issue.

Hello, Canada!
Larry Mann was doing an interview program from Toronto. One night his guests were Jane Mansfield and Mickey Hargitay, her husband. Mann was questioning Jayne about her early career and her financial problems. He leaned forward, starring straight at Jayne, who was, as usual, wearing an extremely low-cut dress, and said, "Tell me, though, Jayne, has there ever been a time when you were flat busted?" Jayne just sat there and couldn't say a word.

Jokers Wild
People in broadcasting have to have a sense of humor to survive April Fool's Day, which brings a rash of pranks to unsuspecting victims. Here is one such case where an unsuspecting weather forecaster was handed the following weather information: "Here's tomorrow's weather forecast: heavy snowfall predicted in the Valley Forge area, which is expected to retard General Washington's troops . . . (OFF MIKE) . . . all right, who's the wise guy?"

Mama Mia!
DISC JOCKEY: . . . and for all of you Cass Elliot fans, here are her big ones on a brand new platter . . . uh . . . here are her big ones . . . er . . . from her brand new album titled 'Mama's Big Ones' . . . (OFF MIKE) . . . whew, that's a mouthful!

By Cracky
The radio station manager, who doubled as salesman and announcer, was reading a commercial for a local grocery store for the upcoming weekend. The fluff he committed went like this: "Remember, ladies, Modern Cash Grocery is featuring special prices for your weekend meal planning . . . And don't forget to stop up on graham crappers."

Truth and Consequences
Ralph Edwards was telling Mike Douglas about the time veteran newsman Lowell Thomas was the surprise guest on "This Is Your Life." The all-too-honest Thomas described the proceedings as a "sinister conspiracy." To make matters worse, the confused Edwards said, "Lowell, I know you are going to enjoy tonight's surprise." To which Lowell snapped back with an annoyed look, "I doubt it!"

No Sex, Please, We're British
ANNOUNCER: "Tonight on BBC, Keith Michell, starring in television's award-winning presentation of King Henry VIII, a dramatization of the life and loves of this provocative monarch and his sex wives . . . *six* wives!"

A Real Pip
A disc jockey on a university campus radio station introduced a recording by Gladys Knight and the Pips with the following: "And now, rock 'n' roll fans, here's a new record by Gladys Knight and the Pimps!"

Just the Facts, Please
On a Dragnet program about an extortionist, Sergeant Friday interviewed a man who had been swindled out of a large sum of money. The man was hesitant to prosecute, because he feared for his family's safety. He nervously told Friday, "You don't understand, I have a wife and three kids, all under twelve."

Daze of the Month
Usually reliable Walter Cronkite drew a complete blank at the close of one of his nightly news programs. He turned to the TV camera, as he had done countless times in the past and said, "And that's the way it is . . . on this . . . what day is this? . . . Oh, yes . . . October sixteenth . . . (laughing) . . . Good-night!"

Hard Headed
Quiz program: "Our next contestant is a Mr. Harwell of Knightsbridge. He works in the meat department of a Safeway Market, where he is the hard butcher . . . I mean he is the *head* butcher!"

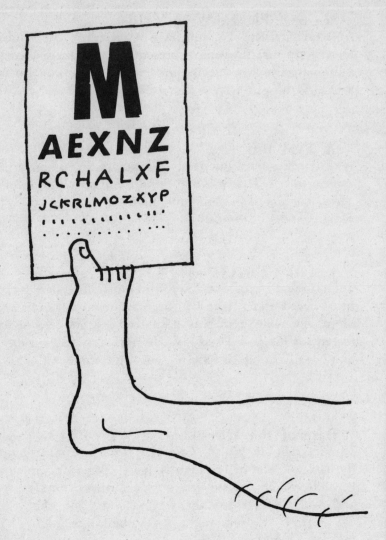

Cockeyed

The host of a local talk show in the mid-west confused his viewers when he told them: "Our next guest is a prominent optometrist, Dr. Harold Levy, who will be talking to us about diseases of the feet."

Learn, Baby, Learn

Consumer crusader Ralph Nader appeared on "The Mike Douglas Show." The conversation centered on Nader's findings concerning alleged false nutrition claims. He said, "For instance, we are looking into some of the claims made by a leading booby foob company." Mike snapped back with, "You had better be careful what you say . . . there may be a lot of boobies watching this show."

Shady Lady

Musical comedy star Carol Channing appeared as a guest with Johnny Carson on his Tonight Show. When it came for him to do a latex paint commercial, he held up the sponsor's product. Carol interrupted to tell how she had used the paint and found it to be very good. Johnny replied, "You see, an ordinary lady we picked up off the street." After the audience roared, Johnny apologized, "Come, now, you know I don't mean that kind of lady."

Blackout

NEWSCASTER: The coal strike is growing worse here in Britain, with more and more workers walking out, and it is expected that the pickets will cause a complete shitdown of the mines . . . that should read *shutdown*. It also appears that sympathetic unions will not cross picnic lines . . . picket lines!

Illegitimate Announcement

Remotes, the programs originating away from the station, give rise to embarrassing and ridiculous situations, such as the time an announcer confidently announced the name of the last selection as "performed by Lex Bastard and his orchestra . . . Lex Baxter!"

A Broad Statement

Christine Jorgenson appeared as a guest on The Mike Douglas Show, after an extensive trip. Mike innocently asked Miss Jorgenson how long she was "abroad," much to the delight of a chuckling audience.

To Your Health

The announcer was doing a commercial for a local drug store, plugging their sale on Vigram vitamins: "So, mothers, give all the members of your family Vigram vitamins to keep them fit and filthy . . . uh . . . healthy!"

Goosy

"The American League standings show the Cleveland Indians in first place with the New York Yankees close up there behind."

Falling Flat on His Ear

Ad libs do not always come off as cleverly as intended. One day, TV's "Galloping Gourmet" decided to "play my next recipe by ear . . . when you are married, it's about the only thing left to play with."

Station Break

Steve Allen was demonstrating the virtues of a non-breakable fibreglass chair on the Tonight Show. The manufacturer had told him to take a hammer and strike the chair as hard as he wished. After the first whack, pandemonium broke loose when he poked a hole right through the chair . . . He bailed himself out by ad libbing: "Well, anyway, this hammer is made of fibreglass."

Open Heart Surgery

D.J. Chris Musk, on Manx Radio, operating in the British Isles, tells the following: A pop version of the well-known hymn "All Things Bright and Beautiful" was going out over the air (artist, Joe Brown). As the record faded, the announcer stated that whenever he went to church services he always looked forward to singing along to the more stirring hymns because one could then "open up your *bowels* and sing forth." The chief announcer immediately phoned in to say: "You open up your heart, not your bloody arse!"

Sour Grapes

Commercial: "So remember, if you have that tired, letdown feeling after a long hot day . . . Welchade Grape is a hell of a way to refresh yourself . . . (PAUSE) . . . you know, of course, this fine drink is a *healthy* way to refresh yourself."

In a Pickle

QUIZMASTER: All right, you have now won fifty silver dollars. Now for one hundred silver dollars, you are to finish the following . . . Are you ready now? Peter Piper-----
CONTESTANT: Pickled Peckers!

Big Man

On What's My Line, Arlene Francis asked the mystery guest if he was a male. Blindfolded guest panelist, Vincent Price, after hearing the guest's voice, chimed in, "All male from stem to stern!"

Have You Got a Wrong Number?

EMCEE: Well, that just about wraps up another Telephone Quiz program for tonight. Tune in again tomorrow at the same time when I'll be crawling on you again!

Sounds Like Dean Martin

During the televised Watergate hearings, former White House legal advisor, John Dean, was questioned about the exact nature of some of his official duties. His surprising answer was: "You might say I was there to make sure all the i's were crossed and the t's were dotted."

Father Knows Best

Pete Wilson, WTMJ-TV Milwaukee, blooped the following: "It has been decided by the city's fathers that all policemen will have their badge numbers sewn on their shorts . . . *SHIRTS!*"

What's in a Name?

A contestant on an audience participation program had the misfortune of being from a suburb of Falmouth, Massachusetts, called Woods Hole. When the host of the show accidently pronounced Falmouth as "foulmouth," the nervous guest tried to correct him: "No, it's *Falmouth,* but actually I'm from Ass Hole, Woodsachusetts."

Paging Mr. Ripley!

NEWSMAN: And now we switch you to Police Headquarters downtown for further developments on the Mary Harkness Case.

POLICEMAN: This is Police Sergeant Edward O'Reilly. The parents of Mary Harkness have asked the police to search for their daughter, who has been missing since 6 P.M. yesterday. She was last seen wearing a blue sweater and gray skirt. Mary is 99 years old and weighs 9 pounds.

From the Chandelier

Veteran Kansas broadcaster Charley Whitworth reports that, on one particularly hectic night at one of the Wichita TV stations, a novice announcer spieled this gem for the Overhead Door Company: "This special on home-type garage doors ends Saturday at five P.M. at the Overdead Whore Company."

Mr. Lucky

Movie actress Honor Blackman was on a promotional tour, plugging the film "Goldfinger" in which she had the role of Pussy Galore. She visited radio and TV stations, where she was interviewed. When she was interviewed on KGO-TV, her enthusiastic interviewer remarked, "I've covered topless bathing suits, bottomless bathing suits, and now I've got Pussy Galore!"

Bad News

NEWSCASTER: Good evening. It's time for the six P.M. news. Tonight's big story is the devastating flood in East Pakistan, brought to you by your Chevrolet dealers.

Could Be

SPORTSCASTER: Before the upcoming New York Jets-Baltimore Colts football championship, scheduled to be played next week at the Super Bowl, Coach Ewbank called his star quarterback, Joe Namath, the most offensive player in football . . . best offensive player.

That'sa Nice

"So for a heavenly Italian dinner, that your entire family will enjoy, try Chef Boy-ar-dee Marijuana Sauce . . . marinara sauce!"

Fore!

The Philadelphia Eagles have a star quarterback whose name is Norm Snead. However, the play-by-play football announcer, an ardent golfer, got his sports mixed up when he observed "Going back to pass to his tight end is Sam Snead."

Splitting Headache

JACK PAAR: (FINISHING COMMERCIAL) . . . so remember, try Bufferin. Boy, do I have a terrible headache . . . I bet I took nine aspirin . . . *Bufferin!!!*

Double Talk

Heard on David Susskind's TV discussion program, "Open End": "I may not always be right, but I'm never wrong."

A Bachelor

ART LINKLETTER: You look like a cute little boy. I would judge you to be around three or four years old. Do you have any brothers or sisters?
BOY: No, I am single.

It's a Treat to Beat Your Meat

A hostess for a daily housewives' hints TV program was talking about the storing of meat in the freezer. After demonstrating how to prepare the meat for freezing, she went into methods for using frozen meat. Her lead-in was: "Now ladies, you take your meat out of the freezer and beat it!"

He's a Scream

SPORTSCASTER: And Joe Namath screams to his tight end . . . uh, that should be *screens,* folks!

Spitz It Out

We wonder what was going on in the mind of the radio announcer who gave his listeners this memorable line: "Stay tuned for an exclusive interview with Olympipic swimming star, Mark Spritz."

Piggy Back
Commercial: "This new Dodge pickup will hold a real pig family . . . that should be *big* family!"

Good Advice
ANNOUNCER: The Mike Douglas Show from Cypress Gardens, Florida, is arranged by the Florida Citrus Commission, who recommends that you start your day off right getting juiced . . . I mean start your day with a glass of Orange Juice.

The Cat's Meow
Johnny Carson had as his guest a woman who ran a cattery—an establishment for the care and sale of cats. Johnny shook up his late night viewers with, ". . . and in a little while we are going to bring out a lady who runs a cat house."

Keeping Up with the Joneses
Ed Sullivan, talking briefly to Jack Jones after his spot on the Sunday night TV program, asked, "Wasn't Alan Jones your father?" "He still is," snapped the Jones boy.

There's Many a Slip Twixt the Cup and the Lip
A London announcer, giving the day's program schedule, blooped the following . . . "At 1:45, London Weekend brings viewers 'University Challenger,' followed at 2:15 by an in-depth leak into the F.A. Cup . . . *look* into the F.A. Cup final . . . I beg your pardon!"

Lousy Weather
WEATHER FORECASTER: The weather forecast for New Orleans and vicinity is partly clousy and tatered shunder towers.

Shut Out

Allen Ludden described one of the contestents on his program, Password, in the following manner: "We now have a female contestant with 33 years of happy marriage, and no score yet . . . uh, in the game."

Odd Couple

While introducing her guest, Jack Klugman, Carol Burnett mentioned that at one time "Jack was Ethel Merman's leading lady . . . ah, leading man!"

Curt Remark

During the 1971 World Series, sports enthusiasts across the country tried to figure out what Curt Gowdy meant when he said, "Brooks Robinson is not a fast man, but his arms and legs move very quickly."

Inside Story

In an interview with astronaut John Glenn, a newsman asked what the toughest part of his training was. Glenn thought a moment, then answered: "That's a tough one, and it's hard to choose one in particular, but if you think of how many openings there are on the human body, and . . . uh, how far you can go in any one of them, you tell me which was the hardest test."

Playboy

A KPHO-TV announcer in Phoenix, Arizona, startled listeners when his voice came over a preview of a Star Trek episode. The preview showed several scantily-clad curvaceous, bunny-type females dancing in a harem-type surrounding, and the local announcer came in with, "Opie joins a secret club on the Andy Griffith Show, next on KPHO-TV."

Sneaky Pete

Listeners must have wondered what the KLOC, California, announcer, Peter Boyle, meant when he gave the weather and marine forecast, and advised about "small crafty warnings."

Hear, Hear!

During the Freedom 7 space shot, two technicians from Houston were overheard by millions of listeners:

FIRST TECHNICIAN: How is it, Charley?
SECOND TECHNICIAN: I don't know . . . I can't hear a thing on this goddamn phone!

Blankety Blank

Station promo: "Monday is inauguration day . . . stay tuned to this channel and see Nixon *swearing* on the steps of the Capitol in Washington."

Getting to the Bottom of Things

When Jackie Joseph was a guest on the Virginia Graham Show, she wore a particularly short dress. When the hostess asked her about it, Miss Joseph replied, "People kept asking me what I was going to wear, and it's the first time I've ever exposed my bottom half . . . I mean my *legs* on television!"

Urgent Needs

When Peter Lawford was doing his "Dear Phoebe" impression of love-lorn columnists on the Mike Douglas Show, he asked for questions from the audience. A fifteen-year-old boy stood up and started to relate the problems he was having with his wife. Douglas cut in and said, "You're only fifteen? You must have married at an early urge . . . age!"

Hair Today, Gone Tomorrow
Commercial: "So remember, Hidden Magic Shampoo puts hair on your body . . . that should be 'Remember, Hidden Magic Shampoo puts body in your hair!'"

X Rated

On a Hollywood Squares program, Joey Bishop was asked to name the various performers who had played in different versions of "Dr. Jekyll and Mr. Hyde" throughout the years. After telling the names of the stars in the first two versions of the film, Bishop concluded with: ". . . and in 1932, Spencer Tracy did it with Ingrid Bergman after the first two virgins!"

The Old College Try

A sports announcer in Buffalo, New York goofed: ". . . and the penalty against Yale brings it back to the Yarvard twenty hard line."

Virgin Territory

An anouncer at WRR-FM, Dallas, Texas, blooped the following: "Tonight see Eugene O'Neill's 'Long Day's Journey Into Night,' brought to you in its original, uncut virgin."

Red, White and Lavender

Steve Allen, substituting for Dick Cavett, decided to take one of the studio cameras out on the street to photograph people. The camera swung around to an old fire station with a flag hanging listlessly in the still air. Allen commented: "And you can tell there's very little wind in New York today by looking at that limp fag . . . uh, flag."

Kuchie Kuchie

Vivacious Latin star Charo appeared as a guest on the Merv Griffin show. She told Merv that whenever she sees him her heart goes "peter peter."

Having a Ball

Performers in broadcasting can sometimes be the victims of unintended double meanings. Such was the case on a popular children's program on BBC radio, entitled Music and Movements for Infants, presided over by the talented and capable Margery Eel. This innocent double entendre perked up listeners' ears and has since become a classic in the world of broadcasting . . . "Today we are going to play a hiding and finding game with music . . . We are going to pretend that you have got some balls and I am going to hide them . . . The music will tell you where your balls are . . . They may be high up on the ceiling . . . or low down on the floor . . . Now stand up and dance around looking everywhere for your balls . . . I hope that you have found your balls . . . Now toss them in the air and play with them."

He Can't See the Forest

A spoonerism is defined by Webster as an unintended interchange of syllables. It was just that type of blooper that cost an announcer his job when he read a promo about a movie starring Forest Tucker.

Double Trouble

Heard on KLIF radio, Dallas: "There has been a rash of armed robberies in the city, five within the past two hours . . . Two short-armed rubbers . . . robbers held up a bank this morning."

Which End Is Up?

The following blooper was broadcast from Cape Kennedy: "This is mission control at NASA. Apollo Fourteen seems to be experiencing difficulty with a low-voltage battery located at the ass end of the lunar module . . . aft-end!"

Relax and Enjoy It
A channel 5, Atlanta, novice announcer shocked his viewing audience with a report that, "a state prisoner has been transferred to the central mental hospital because he is considered to be an encourageable rapist."

A Fish Story
A North Carolina restaurant, The City Shellfish, will never be the same, since an announcer inadvertently read their commercial thusly: "So, come to the Shitty Selfish, I mean Silly Shitfish . . . oh, hell . . . back to the news!"

Slips That Pass in the Night
While doing a commercial for a leading fabric softener, Ed McMahon was supposed to have slid a pin through a diaper, while saying, "See how easy it is to pass through." Unfortunately, when air time came, he stabbed the pin into the diaper and told startled viewers, "See how easy it is to pee through."

Kid Stuff

NEWSCASTER: Dublin police found a smalltime bomb planted in an automobile . . . that should be small time-bomb.

Guest Who's Coming to Dinner?
The hostess of a local women's program was listing a number of easy casseroles for the working mother to prepare, when she began extolling the virtues of these one-dish meals:

"And one of the nice things about these casseroles is that they have wide appeal to many sordid guests . . . that is, *assorted* guests."

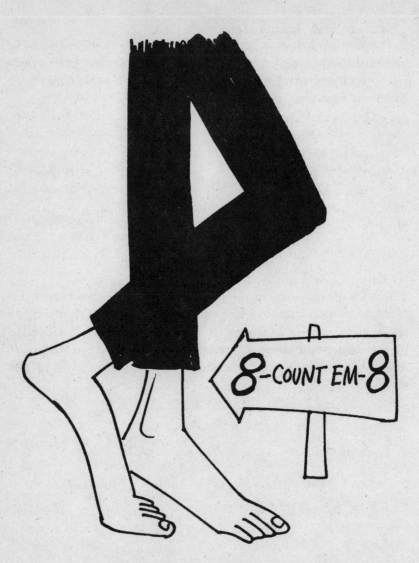

Age Before Beauty

On a popular audience participation program, a pretty young lady contestant was asked for the definition of an octogenarian. She immediately snapped back with . . . "Oh, I know . . . an octogenarian is a person with eight toes."

Nit Picking
Johnny Carson introduced a commercial on the Tonight Show thusly: "And now, friends, we're going to show you how vinyl paneling is tougher than Ray Nitschke of the Green Bay Pickers!"

Come Again?
The armed forces radio network in Vietnam broadcast a story about scientific findings on the Apollo flight to the moon. The announcer read the story as follows: ". . . and the scientists' reports show that the moon rocks may contain living orgasms . . . uh, excuse me, that's supposed to be that the moon rocks have living *organisms*."

White on White
Cousin Duffy, giving weather information on his WMEX Ski Report, said: "And there's a chance of snow mixed with snow later on tonight."

Shop Fast!
Silver Springs, Maryland listeners must have been a little surprised when a local announcer told them to "take advantage of Levitz's sixty-second anniversary sale . . . that is, they've been in business for sixty-two years."

London Bridge Is Falling Down
NEWSCASTER: Queen Victoria was today seen pissing over Westminster Bridge on her way to Buckingham Palace.

Please Be Patient

With the increasing popularity of medical discussion programs, doctors are finding it isn't enough just to be a com-
petent surgeon. Many of them are having to brush up on
public speaking, to avoid Bloopers like the following:

HOST: So how many patients do you think would be the
maximum for one nurse?
DR.: Generally speaking, there shouldn't be more than seven
patients in a hospital bed for each nurse on duty.

With Lox

Station promo: "See the New York Jets play the Cincinnati Bagels this Sunday on NBC . . . I mean Bengals!!"

Good Show

An announcer on the BBC in England told his audience that he had an exclusive interview in store for them. He stated that he was going to present films at 9 P.M. that evening showing him "queering the Queen just before the Coronation . . . I beg your pardon . . . I meant querying the Queen!"

Child Bride

Art Linkletter was interviewing a group of six- and seven-year-olds on "People Are Funny." Coming to one little girl, he asked, "And what age would you like to be?" "Twelve," answered the girl. "Oh, that's an interesting age to be," he replied. "And why do you want to be twelve?" "Because my Mommy's twelve!" replied the little girl. "My," snickered Art, "we sure have some strange marriages nowadays!"

Cross Your Heart

Heard on the morning "Dick Van Dyke Show": "This program has been brought to you by Playtex Loving Bra . . . Living Bra!"

Nuff Said

Playing Stump the Band on the "Tonight" Show, Johnny Carson called on a woman in the audience for her musical selection. When she stood up, she appeared quite large in the midsection.

CARSON: You are?
WOMAN: Yes!

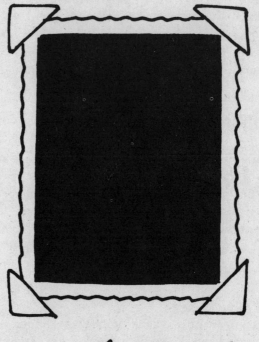

At the Beach —

Get the Picture?
Commercial: "You can get this attractively priced camera at Mel's . . . it's guaranteed to take pictures in either black or white."

Flucked Again
NEWSCASTER: According to Enoch Powell, Member of Parliament from Wolverhampton, the pound will suffer further fucktuation before it stabilizes!

She Hasn't the Foggiest
A BBC woman announcer doing a weather forecast read the copy from the telex, which accidently eliminated the letter "f" in fog. Caught by surprise, she told her audience . . . "I am sorry to have to inform you that there is no f . . . in fog."

Cold Shoulder
An interesting commentary was perpetuated by Britain's own Henry Cooper when he was talking about the controversial Sonny Liston retirement in the world championship fight against Cassius Clay, or Muhammed Ali. Henry remarked that Liston had a "very unusual injury . . . a dislocated soldier!"

Quite a Switch
EMCEE: Our next contestant has a job with a fine newspaper. She is a switchblade operator with the Toledo Broad . . . I mean switchboard operator with the Toledo Blade . . . I beg your pardon, young lady.

Night-mare
Allen Ludden, emcee of the popular television program, "Password," was telling his TV audience about the show's move to another night in the week, when he came out with this classic: "Just remember, folks, next Monday night 'Password' will be seen on Thursday evening!"

Birds Do It

Merv Griffin, on Play Your Hunch, told a visiting guest star, "We sure thank you for taking time out from your busy sexual . . . I mean schedule."

We Heard You the First Time

Election returns: "It is a very close race here in the eleventh district, and it's beginning to look as though Mayor Bailey, the incompetent, will be defeated! . . . (PAUSE) . . . I apologize to his honor, the mayor, the *incumbent*."

Tom, Dick or Harry

Elizabeth Taylor and Richard Burton appeared in an exclusive interview on the David Frost Show. In a serious moment, David queried, "Now that you have all of the material things of life, what do you want most, a baby by Richard?" Liz came back with, "Who else?"

A Good Sport

This sports commentator should have left well enough alone instead of trying to correct himself:

"Good evening, sports fans; we're crammed into a field house where tonight's sexual competition begins, with the State High School championship . . . did I say sectional? . . . I meant sexual."

Smashing!

SPORTSCASTER: And now stand by for a running of the exciting annual race car event, the Grand Pricks. . . er Grand Pee . . . however the hell you pronounce it . . . I'll give you the spelling and you take your choice. Grand P-R-I-X!

Sore Spot

When Hollywood's version of F. Scott Fitzgerald's "Tender Is The Night" finally came to television, one local announcer renamed it.

ANNOUNCER: Tune in at seven tonight for the Channel 5 movie. See Jason Robards in "Tendonitus."

Red Faced

During coverage of a Harvard basketball game, the local sports announcer blurted out the following: "And Harvard keeps on rolling up the score! It looks like nothing can stop the crappy scrimson team . . . er, *scrappy crimson* team!"

The Rain in Spain

DISC JOCKEY: And now we hear the ever-popular "Singing in the wain sung by former Hit Parader, Bea Rain.

Out to Pastor

On his first Sunday "Service of the Air," the young pastor was extremely nervous. The sermon was going well until he came to the tenth commandment and advised both parishoners and radio listeners,"Thou shalt not cover thy neighbor's wife, nor his maidservant, nor his ox, nor his ass."

Air Time

Back in the 1930's, Decca Records had a 78 rpm record release by "Whoopee John and his Orchestra." The record label carried the full name of Whoopee John Wilfahrt, which caused one poor announcer to bloop: "And now, Whoopee John Wilfahrt and the Orchestra will play."

Making an Ass of Himself

This Blooper was contributed by Peter Marshall, host of the Hollywood Squares game show. He was paraphrasing one of Emily Post's rules of etiquette when he said: "When a man is finished smoking a cigar, should he leave his butt in the asstray? . . . I mean leave his butt in the *ash*tray!"

T'ain't Funny, McGee
On the NBC-TV Today Show, Frank McGee was speaking about the Supreme Court decision against capital punishment: "Currently on death row in this country are Sirhan Sirhan, assassin of Robert Kennedy, Richard Speck, who was found guilty of the murder of seven nurses, and Charles Manson of the Sharon Turd mothers . . . Sharon Tate murders."

Moving Story
Tiny Tim was a guest on the Mike Douglas Show, when he told the audience he had lost forty pounds on a diet of onions and prune juice. Host Douglas commented, "Well, that ought to keep you moving." The audience broke up, and Douglas tried to cover the Blooper by saying, "I mean from place to place."

And That's the Way It Is
Even experienced newscasters like Walter Cronkite can make mistakes, as evidenced by the remarks he made after the late President Eisenhower returned from a vacation in Florida: "Apparently the Florida vacation did him a lot of good. Ike returned today looking fanned and tit . . that is, tanned and fit."

One Liner
ANNOUNCER: And now, here's the laugh king of the one-winer, Henny Youngman.

Thrown for a Loss
NBC sportscaster Charles Jones reported to surprised football enthusiasts that Joe Namath was "20 yards underweight."

An Orgy

All action disintegrated into hysterical laughter on the To-night Show one evening, when beautiful, blonde Carol Wayne told Johnny, "I had my first big affair; I had forty people."

A Run for Your Money

ANNOUNCER: Stay tuned for our Late Show movie stars Laurence Harvey and Lee Remick in *The Running Man,* brought to you tonight by Ex-Lax.

Floored!

During NBC's coverage of the 1972 Republican Convention, John Chancellor made reference to NBC's "floorless fear reporters." He attempted to correct himself, but this time it came out "fearless four reporters." Finally he admitted, "I can't say it. I couldn't at the Democratic Convention, either."

Policemen's Ball

Pity the poor newsman who found himself out of a job, after reading this story on the air: "In a concentrated effort to apprehend the rapist, local police have asked all women in the area to copulate with them . . . uh, that is to *cooperate* with them."

Hold That Tiger!

WXYZ-TV Sportscaster, Dave Diles, learned about the pitfalls of live interviews the hard way. After a Detroit Tigers winning game, he went back into the locker room to talk to the celebrating players. He asked Tiger Eddie Brinkman how he felt about the successful game, and was told, "It's a fantastic feeling, not so much for myself, but for the rest of the f---in' guys."

Leave the Driving to Us

NEWSCASTER: Plans were announced for the parade which will follow the Governor's conference. At 2 P.M. the cars will leave their headquarters just as soon as the Governors are loaded.

Doesn't Everybody?

On the popular Art Linkletter program, a youngster was asked what he wanted to be when he grew up. He replied, "A space man." He was then asked what he would do if he ran into a Martian. The youngster snapped back with, "I would say 'Excuse me.'"

Turn On-Turn Off

BBC TV personality David Hamilton followed the custom of reminding viewers to be sure to turn off their TV sets before retiring. "This is David Hamilton bidding you good night, and a reminder for you to be sure to turn off your sex!"

Private "I"

A fast-talking news announcer on WJAC-TV, Pennsylvania, read a story with follow-up information on the murder of union leader Joseph Yablonski:

ANNOUNCER: A .38 caliber revolver was found in the river today by FBA Igents.

One Hundred Percent Pure

Commercial: "So remember these remarkable statistics, and remember Crest, for the family that wants pure cavities!"

That's Rich

Governor Nelson Rockefeller of New York came out with this classic: "Take the typical unmarried woman of this State with three children . . ."

Paleface Speak With Forked-Up Tongue

After an exciting baseball game, the local sportscaster attempted to recap the action, with the following result: "Well, it took eleven Indians to beat the Cleveland innings, today!"

Girl Talk

NEWSCASTER: . . . and Lesbian Forces today attacked Israel . . . *Lebanese!*

The Cold Gray Mare Ain't What She Used to Be

WEATHER FORECASTER: And as we take a look at our weather map, we notice a cooler ass of mare sweeping in from Canada!

Glub Glub

STATION PROMO: "Jacques Cousteau and John Denver will do some unrewarding, er, underwear exploring tonight . . . *UNDERWATER!*"

Sugar and Spice

Mary Margaret McBride, famed radio personality, blooped: "There are many things that you're not supposed to eat, especially children."

Time to Retire

Heard on the BBC: "As Big Ben's cock strikes eleven . . . it's time for the news!"

Vanishing Americans

NEWSCASTER: Here is a news bulletin from our newsroom. The federal government has ordered schools in Mississippi to disintegrate.

I Wonder Who's Kissinger Now

The news writer who put together the following story should have been a little more careful in his phrasing:

NEWSCASTER: On his way to the Vietnam Peace talks, Dr. Henry Kissinger made a stopover in Hawaii, where an attractive island girl gave him a lei.

A House Is Not a Home

The following lively exchange took place on an afternoon audience participation program:

HOST: And now, madame, before we let you select your category, is there anything you need to ask?
LADY: Yes, I'd like to ask you not to call me madame. Where I come from that refers to a woman who runs a house of ill-repute.
HOST: Oh really, madame?

Service With a Smile

Public service announcement overheard on a small New England radio station: "So if you need assistance with your call, just dial one-one-three, and a cheerful call girl will be at your service."

Racy

Joe Croghan, a Miami, Florida, sportscaster, once advised startled listeners to stay tuned for a video tape presentation of the running of the auto racing classic, the Grand Pee.

A New Twist

A lady pretzel baker making an appearance on the Tonight Show demonstrated to Johnny Carson and his late-night viewers the precise method of looping the dough to make the characteristic pretzel shape. Carson attempted to repeat her performance, but the dough didn't come out right. The lady gave him another strip of dough, saying, "Here, try this piece, I don't think yours was long enough. You can't do it if it's not the right length." The audience broke into hysterical laughter, and was just quieting down when Carson quipped, "Yes, I think I've heard that rumor before."

Freudian Slip

NEWSCASTER: On their way to a well-deserved vacation, Hubert Humphrey and Edmund Muskie stopped in Miami, en route to the Virgin Islands, and were visited by President-elect Nixon, who extended his hostility . . . I mean *hospitality* . . . to the defeated candidates.

Dog-Face Soldiers
PUBLIC SERVICE ANNOUNCER: "The local V.F.W. is sponsoring a dance at the civic center this Friday night at 8 p.m. Admission is one dollar per person, and all proceeds will go to the Veterinarians of Foreign Wars."

All Chucked Up
Chuck Conners was a guest on a women's afternoon TV program, when the hostess noticed there were only a few seconds left in which to close the show. She interrupted him with, "Well, I see our time is just about *up Chuck,* so we'll have to save it for the next time."

What's in a Name!
When Grampian Television was being formed in the British Isles, a proposed title was Scottish Highlands and Islands Television. This caused some consternation when one of the owners suggested that station S.H.I.T. would not be appropriate.

Easy? . . . No, Deeficult!
SPORTSCASTER: We have momentarily lost the video portion of our broadcast of the baseball game in which the Minnesota Twins are leading 2 to one . . . as soon as our difficulties are restored, we will resume the broadcast.

Coffee Break
The TV commercial announcer had given the news headlines, then in his juiciest and most churchlike tone he said: "More news in a minute, but first a word from Maxwell House Instant Coffee . . . Be sure to look for the jar with the stars on top . . . if you haven't tried it yet, I envy you!"

A Broad Statement
NEWSCASTER: You have just heard the news from in and around the nation . . . and now to Pauline Fredericks for the latest news from a broad!

Off the Cuff
When Karen and Richard Carpenter were the surprised guests on the "This Is Your Life" show, host Ralph Edwards gave them the traditional gifts given to guests on that program, a charm bracelet and a pair of cufflinks. Due to an unfortunate slip of the tongue, Edwards told the listening audience that the Carpenters would receive . . . "a gold charm bracelet for Karen, and brother Richard will get 'This Is Your Life' handcuffs."

Gay Deceivers?
NEWSCASTER: "United States Treasury Agents have announced their intentions to take a closer look into Swish Bank Accounts."

Sticky Fingers
WFIL radio in Philadelphia gave its listeners this surprising bit of public service information: "So hurry folks, and deposit your letters now. We'll be waiting for your droppings in the box."

Some Like It Hot
Blonde, buxom Carol Wayne wore a very revealing shorts and blouse ensemble on the Johnny Carson Tonight Show. When Johnny asked her if the outfit was considered to be "hot pants," Miss Wayne answered: "Yes, I've always had hot pants."

All Wet
NEWSCASTER: And fire commissioner Randolph Davis reported that his department fire-fighters poured over 2,000 gallons of gasoline on the blaze!

Knock Knock
ANNOUNCER: We have just received word from the courthouse that the jury is still out in the Lucy Brock paternity case, and it now looks like they will be knocked up for the night . . . that should be, locked up for the night!!!

Fares, Please
Commercial: "So get to your vacation spot fast and enjoy every fun-packed minute of it. Don't delay . . . call today and learn how to save money with Trans-American Airlines half-assed rates."

He Has One Tied On
SPORTSCASTER: And in the world of baseball: The Los Angeles Dodgers lead the San Francisco Giants 3-3 after eleven innings . . . I've got two words for this report . . . im-possible!!!

Maybe He Knows Something
ANNOUNCER: Good afternoon, ladies and gentlemen, and welcome to a program of songs sung by guest soprano Martha Bartow, who is a member of the Southern Methodist Glee Club here in Dallas. Miss Bartow is rated as one of the finest swingers here in the Southwest . . . of course, I mean *singers* in the Southwest!!

Trick or Treat

An Associated Press typographical error caused a mid-west announcer to read this unusual story to his listeners: "Many clergymen feel the recent avalanche of obscene material is a treat to young children . . . I'm sorry . . . that's a *threat* to young children!"

Jello, Everybody
Kid's show: "Now, kids, here is the delicious Soupy Sales Advertising Jello, which comes in many hilarious flavors."

Sterling Remark
On NBC's "You Don't Say," emcee Tom Kennedy said to Ann Jeffries, "I know who you were thinking of, Ann, you were probably thinking of your lovely wife, Bob Sterling . . . I mean, your lovely wife, Bob Jeffries."

Strained Remark
On the Merv Griffin Show, Virginia Graham asked Merv and Arthur Treacher if they carry grudges. Arthur Treacher replied that all he carried was a hernia!

A Nose for News
NEWSCASTER: We switch you to England for a report on the latest bombings in Belfast from Ray Sheerer, NBC's nose correspondent in London.

What a Man
SPORTSCASTER: . . . and leading the pike with a one-stroke lead, I mean pick . . . I mean *pack* . . . is Dick Sikes, who has a total of 281 after 54 hores . . . that should be holes!

Oh, Johnny
During one of Johnny Carson's monologues he stated: "You know on New Year's Eve most people are prone (AUDIENCE LAUGHS) . . . not that kind of prone . . . I mean susceptible to liquor!"

On Thin Ice
A confused hockey announcer on CBS's "Game of The Week" blurted out this startling bit of information: "I think he got the stick in the nose. He broke his nose earlier, and it looks as though it's the same nose that he injured before."

No Strings Attached
In an apparent effort to lull his listeners to sleep, Terry Smith of WOCN in Miami, Florida, told his audience to stay tuned for the sounds of "the Bobby Hackett Springs."

A Tight Squeeze
When Johnny Carson introduced his guest, composer Mac Davis, he credited the musician with having "a dozen songs in the top ten."

A Lot of Feeling
Dick Cavett had Dyan Cannon as his guest on his late night show. As she held his hand, he made this comment: "You're very touchy . . . uh, you're very touching . . . you touch a lot, don't you?"

Gave Proof Through the Nyet . . .
NBC's veteran newsman, John Chancellor, was covering President Nixon's trip to Moscow when he made this classic boner. As the President disembarked from the plane at Moscow Airport, a Russian band saluted him by playing the Star Spangled Banner.

CHANCELLOR: And as President Nixon steps down from the plane, a band has begun playing the Soviet National Anthem.

Whatcha Know, Joe

Movie star Joe E. Brown was pinch-hitting for Don McNeil on his ABC Breakfast Club. He interviewed a woman who told him she had four children. "That's your entire family, I suppose." "Hell no, there is a father too," she replied indignantly.

Indecent Exposure

A late night announcer got a call from a female listener who tried to guess what he looked like. After telling the radio audience that she thought the announcer was about six feet tall with sandy hair, she asked him how close she had come. He told her she was very close. Then the lady said, "I think I speak for all your listeners when I say we would like to see you exposed."

Severest Critic

On the TV kid show "TV Art and Crafts," the emcee asked a youngster the following: "Tell me, son, what do you think of your sister's painting?" The boy's answer was direct and to the point: "I think it's crappy!!!"

Bull Thrower

A contestant on "You Bet Your Life" was a bullfighter. He told emcee Groucho Marx that he had met more than three hundred bulls in the ring. Groucho snapped back with, "Young man, you must be the envy of every cow in Mexico!"

Poor Mother

NEWSCASTER: "Governor Nelson Rockefeller today vetoed a bill to repeal New York's 1970 liberalized abortion law, considered the most liberal in the nation. It permits a woman to have an abortion on request within the first twenty-four months of pregnancy."

Quack Quack
Heard on the BBC: "City fathers were hoping to raise enough money to erect a new bronze statue of the Duck of Wellington."

A Live One
ANNOUNCER: This prerecorded program has come to you live from Hollywood.

Bloody Good
Popular band leader Johnny Howard conducted a musical show titled "Easy Beat" on BBC radio for many years. The featured singer was Danny Street, now a popular recording artist. Danny was asked to introduced his next song which was written by Sam Coslow, titled "Everybody Loves Somebody Sometime." Danny blooped . . . "and now for a favorite song of mine and I am sure of yours . . . 'Everybloody Loves Somebloody Sometime.' "

Oral Question

On "Split Second," the quiz show where three correct answers are possible to each question, emcee Tom Kennedy had asked them to finish the next three lines of "Peter, Peter, Pumpkin Eater." A young man who'd just explained that he was a newlywed answered, "Had a wife and couldn't eat her." Somehow, despite the hysteria, the show carried on.

X Marks the Spot
Sunny Ray of KIKK, Pasadena, Texas, was given a commercial at the last moment from the copy department. The spot was for a local outdoor theatre showing an X-rated film where absolutely no one under 18 would be admitted. This is what the listeners heard: "See all three of these big, adult-only features at the Red Bluff Drive-In . . . Absolutely *no one* will be admitted."

Fly Me

On a live network TV drama, the pretty young stewardess on the trans-Atlantic flight had just finished passing out a snack consisting of mixed drinks and assorted salted nuts, when the plane went into some turbulent air. In an effort to calm the passengers, she turned her microphone on and advised them, "We are temporarily experiencing some turbulence, but this should pass in a moment. In the meantime, please hold on to your glasses and nuts."

Knock on Wood

QUIZMASTER: Are you a vegetarian, sir?
CONTESTENT: Oh, no, I'm a carpenter.

Easy Does It!

When Johnny Carson had the sexy Golddiggers as guests on the Tonight Show, he asked who was the tallest, shortest, quietest, youngest. After getting replies from the girls on all those questions, Carson then asked, "And who's the easiest . . ." The audience broke up with laughter before he could complete his sentence, ". . . to get along with?"

Honest John

During coverage of "Operation Cactus," a seizure of several hundred pounds of marijuana at the Texas/Mexican border, John Chancellor read the following interesting material:

CHANCELLOR: There was a really big bust in Texas today, as U.S. and Mexican officials seized more than 500 pounds of marijuana as it was being carried across the border. This was the result of several months of investigation under the auspices of Operation Cactus, which has been described by both Mexican and American spokesmen as a *joint* effort.

Later Than You Think

Miami residents were puzzled when Lynn Russel, a WKAT radio personality, gave the time as "twenty-two minutes past 8:30."

Advance to the Rear

Charo, the vivacious wife of band leader Xavier Cugat, speaks only broken English. However, due to her bubbly personality, she is a favorite on talk shows. When she was introduced to Fernando Lamas on the Merv Griffin Show one afternoon, she shocked the audience, and the worldly Mr. Lamas, when she announced, "Oh, I know all about you . . . I looked up your behind!" As the audience and other guests rocked with laughter, they realized she meant she had looked up his past.

Udder Chaos

Perhaps the news teletype writer could have chosen different words for this story read by Sheila Young over BBC Radio in Bristol, England: "Due to a sudden outbreak of swine visicular disease, all cattle movements have been stopped."

So Long

We wonder if it was a blooper or a Freudian slip when an announcer, who was reading a promotional spot for an upcoming musical program, referred to the violinist (who shall remain nameless) as a *"violin virtuososo."*

Burned Bras

Joey Bishop told his late-night viewers the following: "I was really shocked today. I was on Fifth Avenue, and the Women's Libbers were marching two abreast."

Funny Girl

SPORTSCASTER: Alumnae flocked to the homecoming festivities, and enjoyed a hotly-contested football game, followed by the clowning of the new homecoming queen, Mary Beth Warren.

Homing Pigeon

When actor Walter Pidgeon appeared for a local bond drive, he was greeted by the president of the Drive, who was thrilled at the thought of meeting a movie star. The result of his excitement was the following: "Mr. Privilege, this is indeed a pigeon."

Occasional Pieces

A long-time announcer at WBAT radio in Marion, Indiana, fell victim to a copywriter's mistake, and came out with the following: "Reiger's furniture store features the finest, most durable furniture available. Shop at Reiger's, where we have been servicing the housewife for twenty-six years."

Call a Plumber

ANNOUNCER: Remember that bulk is important to the digestive track to aid in regular movement. Mother should have a good stock of Kellogg's Pep so that you can have a bowl every morning. Yes, kids, be sure Mother is *stopped* up with Kellogg's Pep."

A Sad Tail

Bud Collyer, popular radio and television master of ceremonies, relates the one about one of radio's best known news commentators. The newscaster hadn't gone over his news material in advance this particular evening. He was reading a news item about a prize-winning dog who had been crated and shipped from one city to another. It seemed that the valued dog got his tail caught in the crate. The tail apparently was removed, and the irate owner sued for $10,000 in damages. The commentator unhesitatingly said: "That's a lot of money for a piece of tail." There was a moment of silence while he mulled that one over.

Street Walkers

On the New Year's Eve Tonight Show, Johnny Carson was interviewing some girls who were working in a nightclub that happened to be on strike. The girls were unhappy about the strike, so Johnny asked, "Why aren't you girls out on the streets?" (AUDIENCE STARTS LAUGHING) . . . "What I really meant is, why aren't you picketing?"

Half Dozen of One, Six of the Other

Movie commercial: "Coming next week to the Strand Theatre, lovely Doris Day, starring in "With Sex You Get Eggroll . . . With *Six* You Get Eggroll!"

Pow!

"See the adventures of Bobin and Ratman this afternoon at 4:00 P.M. . . . Robin and Batman!"

Cleansing His Soul

People act strangely when they are near a microphone or a TV camera. A classic example is a porter who went into a BBC studio just after a live transmission. Seeing what he thought was a dead microphone, he walked up to it and declared, "This is the BBC, and this is William Robinson cleaning it." What Mr. Robinson did not know was that the microphone was "live" and that his profound statement was heard during the course of a religious church service broadcast to the nation.

He's Got to Go

Johnny Carson once said on the Tonight Show, "Here's how to relieve an upsex stomach . . . I mean an upset stomach . . . with Sex-Lax . . . Ex-Lax!"

Black is Beautiful

A WNAJ, Mississippi, newscaster got inadvertently mixed up when he read this item about a bank robbery: "Police say a bank in Holly Springs was robbed a few minutes ago. An eye-witness has identified the robber as about 5' 11" and wearing a black ladies' wig . . . uh, lady's black wig."

One on One

Curt Gowdy, reporting the NCAA Basketball finals, confused listeners with this: "Rex Morgan winds up his career today, the only starter in the starting line-up."

How Does That Grab You?

When Joan Rivers hosted the Tonight Show one evening, her guests were Hugh O'Brien and Marty Allen. The discussion was about groupies, and how they fight to get pieces of clothing and locks of hair from their favorite entertainers.

JOAN: Hugh, you're so good-looking . . . did any woman ever try to grab anything of yours?

HUGH: Uh, well . . . (AUDIENCE STARTS BREAKING UP)

JOAN: I mean clothing, silly.

ALLEN: That ain't all they grab!

Affairs of State

NEWSCASTER: Henry Kissinger, President Nixon's whorin' affairs advisor . . . *foreign* affairs advisor, today told newsmen about his latest affair . . . that should read latest lady-friend!

Strange Weather

A weatherman reported, "A line of thunderstorms is moving steadily southweird."

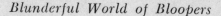

Picture This

Public service messages are frequently read by laymen whose lack of professional training makes them very susceptible to on-the-air Bloopers. Here's an example that was broadcast over a small FM station in the northeast:

"The police department wants young, aggressive men to consider a life in law enforcement. New recruits are given intensive training in handling of firearms, marksmanship, self-defense and finger-painting."

Movies Are Better Than Ever

A female radio personality, who shall remain nameless, advised her listeners of the following: "I saw 'The Godfather' last night, and it was terrific! One of the most exciting films I have ever seen. If you get a chance, go see it, but don't bother buying refreshments . . . you'll never be able to watch popcorn and eat 'The Godfather' at the same time."

Freudian Slip

Heard on Johnny Carson's "Tonight Show":
ED MC MAHON: So stop in at your nearby hot pint dealer for a demonstration . . . I mean your near boy Hotpoint dealer!

From Dixie

Station break: "Stay tuned for a program of jazz, featuring the Dicks of Duxiland . . . I mean the Dukes of Dixieland!"

That's Rich!

When rookie outfielder Rich Chiles was interviewed for the first time on national television, he was understandably nervous. Sportscaster Loel Passe asked him how fast he could run, and got this surprising answer:

"Well, I've run from home plate to first base in under four seconds, which is pretty fast, but of my hits have been to the outfield, so I don't really have to bust my ass . . . that is, I don't really race to first base on hits to the outfield."

Punch Line

A sportscaster at WCAX-TV, Burlington, Vermont, was giving information about the fighting career of Mohammed Ali, when he came out with this delightful spoonerism: "Ali's next *fitle tight* will be held in a few months."

Under Cover Work

On the syndicated game show "Anything You Can Do," host Gene Wood told a contestent, "Now try to pull the blanket out from under you in one swell foop!" After the young lady had completed the stunt, Gene asked her, "Now, Amy, have you ever had so much fun on a blanket before?"

One Way to Score

Heard on KYTV, Springfield, Missouri: "And today, in the National League Pennant Rape . . . Race! . . . the Pissburgh Pirates are on top."

General Disappointment

The accidental deletion of the letter "s" in a news story caused an unsuspecting radio announcer to read the following news item: "The sagging morale of army nurses has been attributed to their dissatisfaction with military bras. I'm sorry, that should be *brass*."

Food for Thought

NEWSCASTER: And word has just reached us of the passing of Mrs. Angela Cirrillio, who died at the age of eighty-seven. Mrs. Cirrilio was a noted amateur chef who specialized in Italian cooking. There are no survivors.

Lordy!

On "The Newlywed Game," the announcer asked this question: "Who will your wife say was the first person to enter your house or apartment?" The husband's answer was "the landlord." When it was time for the wife to answer, she said, "It was my mother-in-law." The disappointed husband said, "I thought it was the landlord." "No, silly. That was before we were married!" said the determined spouse.

Double Meaning

Peter Lawford and Shelley Winters were discussing the selling price Lawford was asking for his beach house.

PETER: It's only a two-bedroom house, Shelley.
SHELLEY: Yes, but they're all so used looking as I remember them. (AUDIENCE STARTS TO LAUGH) . . . I didn't mean that!

Ain't It a Shame

STATION ANNOUNCEMENT: "BBC presents William Shakespeare's 'The Shaming of the Trew' tonight at nine."

Having a Ball

A disc jockey on WHLO, Akron, Ohio, announcing the next record, came up with this Blooper: "And now, here's Gary Lewis and the Playballs . . . uh . . . that's Playboys!"

Wine, Women and Thong

Commercial: "Next time you are entertaining, be sure to have on hand Italian Swish . . . I mean Italian *Swiss* Colony Wine."

Consult Your TV Guide

"See 'Dragnet,' featuring actual criminal cases from the files of the Los Angeles Police Farce, starring Sergeant Thursday, on Friday . . . I mean Sergeant *Friday*, on Thursday."

Fumble

NEWSCASTER ON THE NEWS: "And in the Super Bowl the Pissburgh Spielers beat the Callas Dowboys . . . Dallas Cowboys 21–17."

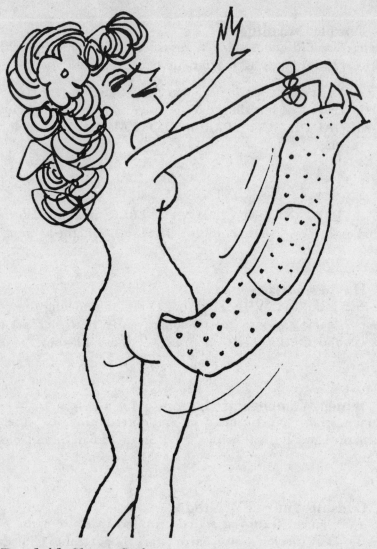

Bandaid Sheer Strip

KBFI-TV, Dallas, Texas, was the scene of a classic blooper, when a member of the six o'clock news team read the following: "A stripper was arrested today in Denton, Texas for wearing only two bandaids during her act. I sure hope they were ouchless." Unable to resist temptation, the anchor man then interjected, "I'm glad you're keeping abreast of the situation."

Wild Pitch!

After a Montreal Expos-Brooklyn Dodgers game, sportscaster Russ Taylor was advising listeners in Montreal about the rest of the major league baseball scores when he made this classic blooper:

". . . and Tom Seaver of the New York Mets pitched a two shit hutout . . . er, two hit *shutout* against the San Diego Padres."

Sic Religious

Years ago, Jack Gregson was a back up announcer for CBS radio. Finally, the time came for him to do his first coast-to-coast live broadcast, a religious program. He introduced a hymn as " 'The Lord Shall Lead His Shock of Fleep,' sung by the Mormon Tabernickle Choir."

Let's Make a Deal

No comment on this used car commercial from a TV station in Indiana:

"Friends and neighbors, we have such a wide selection of new and used cars that we want you to come down right now and make a deal. Bring your wife along and we can *dicker*."

You Can't Take It With You

In an on-the-air obituary on WVMG, Cochran, Georgia, the novice announcer read, ". . . survivors include two dollars . . . (BREAK UP) . . . that is *daughters*."

Loose Talk

DISC JOCKEY: Up next, a very popular song. Here's Andy Williams singing "Can't get Loose to Using You."

Budding Genius
Surprised North Dakota radio listeners were told about an exhibition by a millionaire art connoisseur who would be displaying "the newly-acquired bust of his twelve-year-old granddaughter on TV."

Bull's Eye!
NEWSCASTER: . . . when F.B.I. agents boarded the plane, a fight began. During the struggle, the hijacker's gun went off, wounding a stewardess in the tail section.

The Other Side of Barbra Streisand
"See Barbra Streisand portray Funny Brice in Fanny Girl."

Oh, Rats!
NEWS ANNOUNCER: The rioting hippies were finally brought under control after police sprayed mice into the crowd . . . excuse me, I think that should have been mace!

Cocktail Party
NEWSMAN: Political experts admit that Agnew originally rode into office on Nixon's cocktails, but insist that he will be elected on his own merit in 1976.

Improved Erection
A guest on a late radio show was discussing religious music, when he told the listeners, ". . . yes, well the acoustics of that cathedral have greatly improved since the building's erection in the late 1800's. Apparently much of the sound in those days was absorbed by the voluminous skirts of female parishioners, but nowadays, with the emergence of the mini-skirt, the old organ really goes to town."

Side Effects

While doing a radio play-by-play description of a Red Sox baseball game, Ned Martin made this comment about one opposing player: "Danny, as you know, was hospitalized last week after complaining about chest and sideburns."

Queer Statement

Des O'Connor, popular host of his own television program in England, finished a song, and then read the lead-in to a commercial as follows: "When I sit down to watch television with my husband . . ." A look of horrified amazement spread across his face.

Adults Say the Darnedest Things

When Art Linkletter interviewed Hedda Hopper on a TV program several years ago, he asked about a certain popular male star. The candid Hedda replied, "Oh, he's on his fifth wife now."

That's The Truth!

Bob Barker asked one of his contestants on "Truth or Consequences" what her hobbies were, and she told him she was very active in square dancing. Barker asked if that was all she was active in. The lady replied that she also had five children, and this caused Barker to respond as follows: "I'm sure you were quite active in that, too!"

Friendly Enemies

Merv Griffin, while competing with Johnny Carson for late night talk show ratings, came out with this Blooper: "Two weeks ago the TV Academy gave me a dinner just so they wouldn't have to give me an enemy . . . Emmy!"

Hot Stuff

Maybe the Colonel makes his chicken differently in Illinois, because an announcer in Waukegan told his listeners: "So rush right down to the Colonel's and have some Kentucky Fired Chicken!"

Busted
A D.J. at a top forty station, WRKO, made this apt comment about buxom Bobbie Gentry's latest record, "Now here's the big bust out of the bayou country . . . Miss Boobie Gentry! . . . uh, that's *Bobbie* Gentry."

Honkey Tonk
Johnny Most is the Boston Celtics' basketball radio play-by-play announcer, who occasionally does the sports reports for WHDH. On one particular show, he read the following: "And on the scoreboard in the National Honkey League . . ."

Misery Loves Company
Johnny Carson was doing a bit on the "Tonight Show" called "Misery is . . .", when one of the gags came out this way: "Misery is having the funny feeling that while you are undressing, a guy is looking at you through his bernockerlers! binockillers . . . a telescope!!"

Lust for Life
ANNOUNCER: Ladies, does your husband wake up in the morning feeling lustless . . . er, listless?

Color Him Yellow
Back in 1957, Mel Venter had a live radio program called "The Breakfast Gang," broadcast from San Francisco. He had a seven-year-old boy on as a guest one day, and he made the mistake of asking the boy, "Would you describe me to the radio audience?" After spending a few minutes telling the listeners about Venter's clothes, the little boy revealed to the audience that, "He has big ears." The laughter had almost died down from that one, when the boy came out with, "And he has yellow teeth."

No News Is Good News
The nation of Zambia has a growing broadcast industry, with many new announcers who have only recently learned to speak English. Our short-wave monitor picked up this classic Blooper:

NEWSCASTER: And now, here *are* the news."

Snow Job
WMEX Radio in Boston used to feature a Ski Report handled by Cousin Duffy, a staff announcer. One memorable afternoon, Cousin Duffy told his listeners: "If you ski in Massachusetts, you'll find excellent conditions in Connecticut."

Nudie
On KOA, Denver, a newscaster told his audience, "Rita Hayworth is now resting on a Nevada Nude Ranch."

Tricky Dick
A young woman on the Dick Cavett Show was discussing women's liberation with her host, when she said she felt sorry for the women who were trying so hard to change things, because they "don't have the same apparatus as men do." The audience broke up and Cavett tried to cover the error by saying, "She means they don't have the same tools." It was quite a while before things calmed down again.

What's Up, Doc?
Apparently the writer was responsible for a classic blooper that occurred on the Marcus Welby program on January 4, 1972. Dr. Welby demonstrated his keen medical perception during a conversation with his son-in-law. They discussed Welby's daughter's pregnancy, and the good doctor advised the son-in-law, "Well, at least you're over the hump."

Jet Stream

NEWSCASTER: Word has just reached us that the B.E.A. 'Go-slow' is ended with a settlement of the work-to-rule by pilots of the British Urine Peean Airways.

Foggy Notion

WEATHER FORECASTER: As I look out the window, I hesitate to say that it is raining, as the weather bureau doesn't call it that. They call it fog. This is to tell you that the fog is overflowing the sewers!

Nervous Wreck

News item: ". . . and after examining the wreckage of the two automobiles, police told reporters it was a miracle that none of the passengers suffered injuries or serious death."

Uplifting Music

A disc jockey at WSAI, Cincinnati, announced a song by Harper's Bazaar in the following manner: "We now hear the 59th Street Bridge Song by Harper's Brassiere!"

Anyone Can Play

On ABC's popular game show, "Password," host Allen Ludden told a surprised contestant, "Come on over and play with Michael Landon . . . (AUDIENCE LAUGHTER) . . . Well, you know what I mean!"

A Case of Booze

As the district attorney on "The Edge of Night" gave his opening statement to the jury in a murder trial, he looked at them very seriously and said, "I am going to be very careful and build this step case by case."

Blushing Bride

The Newlywed Game has been the scene of numerous Bloopers. One of the real classics occurred when a young husband was asked, "What have you done since your wedding that you thought was funny, but your wife didn't?" After thinking it over for a minute, the husband said his wife was afraid of spiders, and that he had put one in the shower one day. His wife went in the bathroom, screamed, and ran out naked. A few minutes later, when the wife was on stage and heard about the question, she turned to her husband and said, "That doesn't count . . . that was *before* we were married!" Her face turned red as the audience broke up. She said, "I hope my mother isn't watching."

Strictly Legit

On a pre-Christmas program, Johnny Carson told his "Tonight Show" viewers: ". . . and now I am going to read some letters from legitimate children . . . (AUDIENCE LAUGHTER) . . . c'mon now, you know what I mean!"

Out of This World

When astronaut Wally Shirra appeared as a guest for an interview on "Meet The Press," panelist Lawrence Spivak asked, "How does it feel to be in a state of wastelessness?"

Watch Your P's and Q's

Don Wardell on Radio Luxemburg's "Music In The Night" late show blooped: "And back from the news we come to 'Fever' from Leggy Pee . . . folks, Peggy Lee."

Double Jointed

George Jessel, star of "Here Come the Stars," told Steve Allen, who was a guest on the program, "You know . . . not too many people know this, but years ago I was the bat boy for the New York Joints . . . Giants!"

Star Player

SPORTSCASTER: And from here in the press box it appears that Bart Starr, the great Green Bay Packer quarterback, had the wind knocked out of him, for which we are most grateful.

Wild Plug

Joey once made this Blooper on "The Joey Bishop Show": "Shelley Winters can be seen wild in the streets . . . (LAUGHTER) . . . in the movie, I mean."

America First

When Mrs. Eleanor Roosevelt visited England during the war, Britons were interviewed for their reactions. Wynford Vaughan Thomas asked one interviewee on a street in London, "How do you think she will be received?" He replied, "With all the heartfelt fervor of a brother nation struggling for its survival." "Are you hoping to see her yourself?" "Alas, no, I understand that only the United States Forces in this country are going to have intercourse with her."

Open Door Policy

When Governor Rockefeller criticized Mayor Lindsay's handling of the New York City garbage strike, Lindsay wanted to broadcast a rebuttal. He assumed the speech was being taped for later broadcast, and did not know his words were going out over the air live when he said: "The city will, of course, endeavor in every way to remove the dangerous accumulation of trash from the sidewalks and streets. I will have a full report for the people in a news conference from City Hall tomorrow. (LOUD NOISE FROM BACKGROUND) We've got to do it again . . . the f---in' door was open."

Sticky Situation

Even the President of the United States can be the victim of a Blooper. In a nationally televised speech about the economy, Richard Nixon warned the public: "We are preaching a gospel of goo . . . er . . . glue . . . gloom!"

Ten Feet Tall

Sportscaster Bill Derne, broadcasting the Miami-Georgia Tech football game, blooped, ". . . and now coming into the game is the five-ton junior from Canton, Ohio."

No Time Like the Present
ANNOUNCER: At the chime it will be the correct time.

I Beg Your Pardon!
Chris Musk, disc jockey at MANX radio, Isle of Man, interviewed me in connection with my first Decca PARDON MY BLOOPER record album release in England, for his "Summer Sunshine" radio program. Chris had been vaguely familiar with my American Blooper record albums and books. In the spirit of politeness he blooped: "Kermit, I have always enjoyed your bloomers!"

Whoops!
The folowing was heard at the beginning of the Jet-Colt football game at the Super Bowl. A statistical comparison between the two teams appeared on the screen. Commentator Curt Gowdy said, "To give you a better idea of how the teams shape up against each other, we'll be throwing up statistics like these all during the game."

Good Timing
Station WKTY, La Crosse, Wisconsin, broadcasts a prayer at noon each day. One day the tape of the prayer was started too early, and when the announcer finally realized his mistake, he simply shut it off and went on with his own announcements. The result was: "The angel of the Lord declared unto Mary . . . the time is now 11:25."

Good Heavens!
Art Linkletter asked a little boy what was the best way to go to heaven. The answer? "Die!"

New Dance Craze

Newscasters covering rocket launchings sometimes put in very long hours, and, as a result, are not always as alert as they should be. One such announcer was trying to fill in with talk while waiting for a film to be shown, when he blooped: "In just a moment we'll be showing you a film of the Moon boogie . . . uh, that is Moon *buggy!*"

Screwed Up

On a radio discussion program, the host and his guest, a labor expert, were talking about factories and assembly lines. The conversation went like this:

HOST: They're finding out that the mass production line is causing too many rejects.

GUEST: Well, what I think it is, too, is the dullness.

HOST: That's right, and the other thing is that we've got a lot of young guys working in the automobile factories who don't dig this screw all day long . . . one screw, one screw, one screw.

GUEST: That's right.

HOST: And they're bored with the job, and any way they stick it in is okay.

I'm Just Wild About Harry

When Harry Belafonte was a guest on the Mike Douglas Show, he talked about his family and told Mike, "I have several children, the oldest twenty-four." Mike then asked Harry how long he had been married, to which Belafonte replied, "Seventeen years." As Mike began counting on his fingers, Belafonte said, "Hey, I've been married before!"

Let's Be Frank

DISC JOCKEY: And now we hear "It Was A Very Good Year" by the chairman of the broad, Frank Sinatra.

Marry the Girl!

The emcee of "The Newlywed Game" asked the husbands what one thing put down their male ego before they were married. One happy groom came up with, "When she said we would have to wait until we got married!"

Out of the Mouths of Babes

"Howdy Doody" for many years has been—and still is—one of TV's most durable and popular kid shows. Talented Bob Smith, who plays Buffalo Bob, interviewed a youngster who floored him with his honest answer:

BUFFALO BOB: What's your name, little fella?
KID: Kenneth.
BUFFALO BOB: And did you do anything wrong?
KID: I farted!
BUFFALO BOB: I see.....
(BUFFALO BOB BURSTS INTO UNCONTROLLABLE LAUGHTER AFTER BEING DESTROYED BY THIS FIVE-YEAR-OLD.)

Pitch Man

A local announcer was doing the sports report for his radio station, when he Blooped the following: "Ted Williams is certain that his middle team will be hitting soon, but his main concern now is the men that his pishers . . . pissers . . . that is, pitchers, keep putting on base."

From Bed to Worse

A Virginia announcer was doing a radio promotion for a department store that had Chris Hanburger of the Washington Redskins available to sign autographs for fans. What the listeners heard was, "Stop by Leggett's to eat Chris Hanburger, Defensive Team Captain and Linebacker for the Washington Bedskins . . . MEET!"

A Bag of Wind

WEATHER FORECASTER: And the latest report from the United States Weather Bureau advises us that typhoid Ida is now threatening the Philippines! . . . typhoon Ida!

Thanks a Lot

Former Governor John Connally of Texas defended Spiro T. Agnew thusly. "Future events will prove him guilty . . . INNOCENT!"

All Wet

Don Dive, British Decca record album promotion man, tells about the disc jockey who played a recording by "The Living Strings," titled, "I Guess I'll Have To Hang My Tears Out To Dry." However, the radio audience heard this Blooper: "And now we spin another record . . . this time we hear The Living Strings playing, 'I Guess I'll Have To Hang My Dreams Out To Dry.'"

Good Ears

Back in the days when dramatic programs were produced live on radio, Bloopers were commonplace. For instance, one time the writers of the Lone Ranger Show were trying to indicate in the script that the townspeople, who were trapped in a cave, were about to be rescued by the famous masked man. Radio listeners heard one character, supposedly holed-up in the cave, deliver this immortal line: "Listen . . . I hear a white horse coming!"

Out of Sight

NBC-TV's John Chancellor told of a rash of recent UFO sightings. A woman who swore in a TV interview that she had seen unidentified flying objects, was asked how she could be so sure that they were, in fact, unidentified flying objects. She confidently replied, "They had the letters 'UFO' on the side."

Slice of Life

One of Johnny Carson's guests on the Tonight Show was an actor who spoke of his bad luck with women. He told Johnny he had invited a girl over for dinner and she stayed for three months. Then he added, "But she was a good cook." Johnny replied, "Three months! She must have made good bed . . . bread!"

Fly Us

NEWSMAN: The hijackers allowed all passengers to leave the plane safely, leaving only the pilot, co-pilot and a coo of troo screwardesses.

Bank Night

Open mikes can be treacherous. Here is a case where a listener phoned a disc jockey several times, inquiring if the banks were open on Veterans Day. In disgust, and believing his mike was not open, the disc jockey came out with . . . "If he is so concerned with the banks being open, why doesn't the son of a bitch call the banks himself!"

Odd-ities in the News

Heard on the NBC-TV Today program: "Since we have been on television, we have had fifty odd Senators and Representatives on our program!"

Screwed Up

Taped from WMAL, Washington: "President Nixon says that the model cities program is better than the *ineffuctive* urban renewal program."

Curt Remark

When Curt Gowdy was giving the play-by-play description of the second game of the 1973 World Series, he surprised baseball fans everywhere with this statement: "Willie Mays won't start today, because the Mets' regular outfielder, Rusty Slob, will be playing. Wait, that's Rusty *Staub!*"

Late Returns

WNBC-TV in New York City ran a spot during their 7:00 to 7:30 news show, which advised listeners to tune in later that night for results of the Democratic run-off between Beame and Badillo . . . a race which had taken place a month earlier.

What a Grouch!

A contestant on Groucho Marx's "You Bet Your Life" TV program indicated that he and his wife had sixteen children. Groucho asked, "Why do you have so many children?" The man replied, "Because I like my wife." After a pause and a particularly long drag on his ever-present cigar, Groucho said, "I like my cigar, too, but I take it out sometime!"

Face Saving Device

A sportscaster at WSBK-TV was covering a Boston Bruins Hockey game when he came out with the following: "Here's Hodge on a breakaway! He's all by himself . . . he shoots . . . and Hodge missed the goal!! He'll be thinking about that one for a while. Just look at the expression on Hodge's stick!"

No News Is Good News

Radio station KTAC, Washington, was the site of an unusual newscast. The regular newscast music finished up, and the announcer came in with, "And now the news at this hour . . . (LONG PAUSE) . . . Where the hell's the news? . . . Christ, where's the news?" For the next sixty seconds, listeners heard only the sound of the announcer laughing.

Hair Apparent

Bloopers are not just limited to American radio and TV stations, as Channel 7 in New Brunswick, Canada found out. A dandruff commercial was not quite finished, when a second commercial cut in with:

"Risdan was made to control dandruff, and does control dandruff. How can you improve on that? . . ."
". . . (CUT IN WITH CARMELITA POPE) . . . Spray it with Pam! Also good for frying pans."

Cool, Man

David Hartman was interviewing Burt Reynolds on the ABC
Good Morning America Show, when he blooped the following.
"We'll be back with Burt in a moment after this word from
General Fools Crude Whip . . . Cool Whip!"

Grapes of Rath

Merv Griffin, host of his own popular talk-show, was describing a famous movie star on his program, but could not recall
the man's name. He was getting more and more frustrated
with himself, then suddenly he remembered the celebrity's
name, and blurted out, "Rasil Bathbone!"

I'll Drink to That

An Illinois announcer who had had one too many before he
went on the air with his regular sports and weather show,
committed a classic Blooper. After tripping over a cable, he
sat down in front of the camera and reported: "The game
between the Chicago Cubs and the St. Louis Cardinals was
rained out because of rain. The forecast for tomorrow's game
will be mostly light with a few scattered sours."

New Wrinkle

"Gambit," a popular CBS game show, offers many prizes to
it's contestants. One morning, the announcer was describing
a sewing machine that was to be given away, when he informed the audience that it "never needs ironing . . . of
course, I mean oiling."

Playing with Themselves

SPORTSCASTER: And now stay tuned for the wrap-up of
the hookey game just played between the Rangers and the
New York Rangers.

Baby Talk

Prescott Robinson of Channel 4 TV in Miami, Florida, gave the youth movement unexpected support when he read this news item: "Illinois is one of the last remaining states to approve voting rights for eight-year-olds."

That Sinking Sensation

A San Jose, California TV station had scheduled the movie "Up Periscope" to begin right after the 5:30 newscast. Perhaps the announcer was a former navy man, because, as the news ended, viewers heard him say, "Stay tuned for the six o'clock movie, 'Up Your Periscope!'"

An Athletic Supporter

There's a club for jockeys in Los Angeles, called the "Jock Trap." The day after one of the KMPC's announcers had interviewed jockeys at the club, he went on the air and told his listeners about the great interviews he had gotten at the "Jock Strap."

Here, Here!

In America, the word "boobs" has an entirely different meaning than it does in England. "Boobs" are commonly referred to as female breasts. In England, the word is synomymous with broadcasting fluffs. Imagine my consternation when I visited BBC Radio One in London for an interview and spoke with BBC commentator, Marion White, who volunteered the information that she had some "lovely boobs" to tell me about.

Air Time

When Gene Klavan was a young disc jockey, he was half of the team "Klavan and Finch" on WNEW in New York. One morning, while Gene was reading a commercial for a clothing store that was featuring windbreakers, he ad-libbed, "These jackets are guaranteed to break any wind." His partner, Finch, started giggling loudly, and Klavan still not realizing what he had said, made matters worse by insisting, "What are you laughing at?"

It Only Seems Like That

ANNOUNCER: This year, the government is issuing new forms for your Eternal Revenue Tax . . . uh . . . that's *Internal!*

Screwed Up

Sailors know that the word "screw" refers to the propeller part of a boat engine. Apparently the word threw the announcer for the game show, "Concentration," Hugh Downs, as he described one of the prizes, a beautiful motor boat. He was supposed to say "the motor has twin screws for pleasure cruising and fishing." What came out, however, was: "the motor has twin screws for pleasure screwing and fishing."

Tricky Dick

An NBC Special News Report informed the public that, "President Nixon has been hospitalized for a virile ailment . . . uh, *virule* pneumonia."

Super Fruit

Many listeners of WMAQ in Chicago were not aware that the announcer was leading into a Nectarine commercial, and were surprised to hear him say: "It won't be long before one of California's finest fruits disappears from your supermarket . . . (GIGGLES) . . . Of course I don't mean that kind of fruit . . . I'm talking about fruit fruit!"

The Duce to Pay

Norman Rosenman, who has been around broadcasting for a numbers of years, reports overhearing this unusual movie promo: "Stay tuned for the movie of the week, Irma La Douche."

Fairy Nice Program

STATION BREAK: "Stay tuned for the Word Quiz Show, sponsored by your local Dairmont Fairy . . . I mean, Fairmont Dairy!!!"

Prevents Accidents

ANNOUNCER: This special network presentation on abortion is brought to you by Goodyear Rubbers . . . Goodyear Rubber Tires!

Put Up Your Dukes

When the Duke of Bedford appeared on Merv Griffin's popular talk-show, he told a humorous story about several of the bedrooms in his mansion, while keeping quite a straight face. After he had finished, Merv commented, "How can you tell a funny story like that with such a bed-pan expression?" The audience broke up.

This Is a Raid!

Heard on WCBS Radio news in New York City: "Other stories in the news . . . Raiders Naders . . . oh God! . . . it should be *Nader's Raiders,* turned their attention to beat selts in automobiles."

Atsa Right

When Nipsy Russell was a guest on the popular game show "$10,000 Pyramid," he had to give clues to contestants about secret words or phrases. One of these phrases was "Tin Pan Alley," so Nipsy gave the clue, "The place where all songs are written." The audience broke into laughter when the nervous contestant replied: "Italy."

The Blooper Spirit

A network newsman read the following item about Howard Hughes:

ANNOUNCER: It appears that mystery man Howard Hughes has landed in England and has gone into hiding at the Inn-On-The-Park Hotel. Reporters were told that the aging millionaire would have to appear personally to renew his passport if he chose to stay in London, but no other information was forthcoming from the Hughes spooksman.

Shorts Subject

Perhaps the copywriter could have used better phrasing when he wrote this story and handed it to the unsuspecting announcer:

"Female employees of the firm went on strike today, alleging that the company is ultraconservative and will not tolerate the wearing of hot pants by its employees. The women also stated that anyone wearing hot pants to work must take them off or face immediate dismissal."

Undercover Man

Wilson Hatcher of Channel 41, Louisville, Kentucky, read the following movie promo: "Be sure to see 'Pretty Maids All In A Row,' headed by Rock Hudson and directed by Roger Vadim, the man who uncovered Brigitte Bardot and Jane Fonda."

Lover Boy

When a South Carolina disc jockey advised his listeners about who was up for Oscar nominations, he surprised them with this unintentional fluff: "And Richard Castellano received a nomination for best supporting actor for his performance in 'Livers and Other Strangers.' "

C'mon Down

The exclusive hotel which bought air time on a yankee radio station was trying to lure cold northerners down into the Florida sun. But they probably didn't get too many takers when a New Jersey announcer blooped the following: "The elegant penthouse of this luxurious, twenty-seven story resort hotel provides an expensive view of the Miami Beach waterfront . . . *expansive!*"

What's Cookin'?

Listeners in Lafayette, Indiana were shook up when the local station ran two commercials back-to-back, with this unappetizing result:

". . . What are you going to get from Burger Chef? What are you going to get, today?"
". . . pimples, blackheads, and acne are problems that plague teenagers everywhere."

It Never Fails

When a Chicago news announcer blew his lines several times on the air, he slammed down his copy and yelled "Goddamnit!!" The panicky director blacked out the regular picture, and put up a slide that said, "Please stand by, Network failure."

Something Not Kosher Here

NEWS ANNOUNCER: The victim of the dog attack, a four-year-old girl, was rushed to the hospital where doctors began the series of shots that will protect her from rabbis . . . uh, that is, rabies.

A Pregnant Thought

A University of Iowa student announcer learned how much damage a copywriter can cause, when he read the following public service announcement on the campus station:
". . . and all U. of Iowa students are invited to attend there will be, er . . . invited to attend. (PAUSE) There will be volleyballswimming, that is, volleyball *and* swimming, softball-badminton, and two live rock bands plus a lot more fun for you and your friends. Boy, the copywriter sure muffed this one, huh? Let's see, she left out one . . . two . . . three . . . four commas, and she missed a period, too!"

The Oys of Texas Are Upon You

Heard in Dallas, Texas: "A peculiarity of the young militants in this Arab/Israeli conflict, is the frequency of their emertional outboasts . . . emotional outboats!"

Pot Luck

The following occurred on a morning ladies audience participation show. Each day there is so much money put into a jackpot and they try to get a winner for the day. They had been unsuccessful for the past few days, so there was a goodly sum in the jackpot. The emcee, after a couple of the usual salutations, said ". . . And as you know, ladies, the crack-pot hasn't been 'jacked' yet."

Doing the Breast Stroke

After a commercial during a movie on Chanel 7 in Chicago, the announcer said, "And now we return to Jane Russell under water . . . I beg your pardon, I meant Jane Russell in 'Under Water.'"

The Eyes of Texas Are Upon You

STATION BREAK: "This is KTIW, Sexas Titty . . . er Texas City."

Everything Half Off

The Quick Trip grocery store advertises on KTUL, Tulsa, Oklahoma. Unfortunately, one of the announcers read a live piece of copy that came out this way: "This portion of the news is brought to you by Quick Strip grocery store, where we can service your every need."

Here Comes the Bride

Richard Whitely, an announcer on England's Yorkshire Television show "Calendar," was doing a special program celebrating the Queen's silver wedding anniversary. He interviewed
a young couple who had come straight from their registry
office wedding to the studio. When he asked the blushing
bride what it was like to be married, she unblushingly replied,
"I can't say . . . it hasn't sunk in properly yet."

Frug It!

Tom Adams of WIOD in Miami, Florida, reported this classic boner made by a fellow announcer: "The recalling of several thousand cans of mushrooms believed to be infected with botulism, was ordered today by the Dude and Frug Administration."

Hang Up

Back in the old days of radio, Shep Fields was broadcasting his "rippling rhythm," featuring Jerry Shelton on the accordion. When Jerry walked up to the mike, the announcer said, "Jerry, what is that big wrinkly thing you have hanging on you?" It broke up the band and audience.

Take Your Choice

Curt Gowdy, broadcasting a play-by-play account of the All Star Baseball game, gave listeners the final score: "And at the game's end, it's National League Six, American League Four. That score again is American League Six and National League Four."

Out to Launch

NEWSCASTER: And a disappointed nation heard the glum news that the United States has suffered another setback in the space race. It is becoming quite apparent that our country is more and more gaining a reputation for its space failures rather than for its accomplishments. No further announcements pertaining to any new rocket launch attempts are expected from rocketeers at Cape Carnival for some time . . . I mean Cape Canaveral.

It's a Corker

Commercial: "So, for those who think young, be sure you're stacked up with a Pepsi Sex pack . . . stopped up . . . stocked up with a Pipsi six pack."

One Too Many
STATION BREAK: "It is now nine P.M., Eastern Standard Time . . . On behalf of all of the personnel here at this station, we want to wish all our viewers season's greetings and a very happy and preposterous new year . . . hic!"

The Price Is Right
Political speech: "And if I'm elected, I can promise you the finest local government that money can buy!"

Who's on First
A TV station in Lufkin, Texas, went off the air for several hours because of transmission difficulties. A hand bearing this hastily-scrawled message appeared on viewers' screens: "We have temporarily lost our slide informing you that we have temporarily lost our picture. Please bear with us!"

Horsing Around
Every British commentator dreads state occasions featuring the Royal Horse Artillery. More than one has described them as "the Queen's Troop of The Royal Arse Hortillery."

Ballin' the Jack
From Jack de Manio's book "To Auntie with Love" comes this gem. Two young ragamuffins had strayed into the BBC's Overseas premises at Bush House in the Strand. No one knows how they got there, or what they thought they were doing. All that was ultimately known was that while the news reader was holding forth to the rest of the world these two urchins, having decided to take a left turn rather than a right, burst into the news studio, crept up behind the news reader and shouted, "BALLS TO THE BBC!" They then vanished out the door.

House of Ill Repute
NEWS ANNOUNCER: The trial of the two prostitutes continues tomorrow at the Corny County Cathouse . . . uh, that is the Cory County Courthouse!

From Out of the Blue
On a dreary, overcast day, a weather forecaster in Washington blooped the following: "And this evening, we will have some miserable precipitation . . . uh, that should be *measurable* prepisitation!"

Hair Raising Blooper
On the afternoon soap opera, "As The World Turns," which was live, one of the actors was having an emotional confrontation with his TV "daughter," when his toupee slowly slid right off his head, unbeknownst to the poor fellow!"

Lost His Head
Overheard during the broadcast of a Miami Dolphins pro football conference game: "Paul Warfield ran a beautiful post pattern, putting his body between himself and the defenders."

Take It Off!
Educational TV: "And now, class, we come to the moment you have all been waiting for . . . a strip film . . . oops . . . I mean a film strip on farming!"

Making Ends Meat
Larry Blyden, hosting *What's My Line,* had two young girls as his next contestants. Blyden gave the customary hint to the panelists, by telling them that the girls "work after school and on work ends."

In the Groove

Foster Brooks, the delightful perennial TV drunk, guested on The Tonight Show, on which John Davidson was the guest host. Brooks told of his days as a straight announcer in radio, and about the incident when he left the studio with a religious program on the air that was pre-recorded. He went downstairs for a quick cup of coffee. When he returned he learned that the needle got stuck. All that the listeners heard was "Jesus Christ, Jesus Christ, Jesus Christ, Jesus Christ . . . !"

Line Forms to the Right

Here's a beaut from a Vero Beach, Florida, radio station: "Mrs. Rosemary Richey, Supervisor of Erections, has announced that her orifice . . . OFFICE will remain open Saturday night for late applications."

How Does that Grab You

The following was heard by viewers watching the Detroit Channel 7 news program. Newscaster Jack Kelly announced: "The meat you buy in the supermarket will look the same, taste the same, and cost the same, but will not *be* the same because the USDA has changed the way butchers grab their meat . . . er . . . *grade* their meat."

Queer Remark

During the 1975 AFC playoff game between the Baltimore Colts and the Pittsburgh Steelers, Don Meredith blooped when he said this of Baltimore coach Ted Marchibroda: "I've met him, and he seems like a really nice gay . . . GUY!!"

Wanted Dead or Alive

NEWSCASTER: "Officials are still trying to locate two miners who are trapped in the mine shaft. They don't know if the men are still dead, or if they are alive. . . . (OFF MIKE) . . . The news department sure gave *me* the shaft on this one!"

What a Gas!

A newscaster on WWCH, Clarion, Pennsylvania, gave his listeners quite a shock when he read the following news story: "Yesterday, 7000 peasants suffering from encephalitis, a type of sleeping sickness, were gassed to death in New Hampshire . . . that should be *pheasants!*"

Who's Fooling Who?

On a local news program, a little girl was being interviewed about her father, who was serving in Vietnam at the time. The conversation went like this:

GIRL: Daddy always used to fool around and call me his only girl.
ANNOUNCER: What did your Mommy say about that?
GIRL: Nothing. She used to fool around, too.

Ups and Downs

A New Hampshire announcer's mind was obviously not on his work when he gave the daily stock market report which included the following information: "After a fast increase this morning, Wall Street storks dropped nine pints on the Dow-Jones averages."

They're Not Bored

In a news story carried on Channel 4 TV in Miami, the following was heard: "In addition to their small salaries, the migrant workers are usually given bread and broad . . . uh, that is bed and board."

I'll Drink to That!

When one of England's Members of Parliament decided not to run for re-election, television cameras were on the scene for his unforgettable statement: "Having *swerved* in the House of Commons for nearly two decades, I feel it time to step down."

Something Not Kosher Here

Commercial: "Remember, for this week only, Food Fair is featuring a Passover special on Rath bacon and ham."

Honest John

When "Those Magnificent Men in Their Jaunty Jalopies" played on a Georgia TV station, a commercial cut in when Tony Curtis was proposing to his girl friend. What listeners heard, was: "And if I win the race, I will find you, get down on one knee, and say . . . (CUT IN) . . . Does your toilet bowl need cleaning?"

Truer Words Were Never Spoken

Garry Moore, host of the popular "To Tell The Truth" show, introduced a commercial this way: "Now we pause for an outrageous commercial . . . uh . . . a courageous commercial . . . sorry."

Holy Mackerel!!!

When I returned from London, after several appearances on BBC television and radio in connection with the release of my books and record albums throughout England, I was greeted at the airport by April Kelly, my girl friday, who told me that she had some perplexing news. The post office had contacted our office to advise us that they had received a stack of books which we were to pick up. This mysterious shipment came at a time when my previous book, Best of Bloopers, had just been released by Avenel Books. We headed directly to the post office from the airport. Upon opening one of the packages, we saw the "Best of Bloopers" covers. April opened one of them up, only to find that the bindery had made an error. Within the Blooper covers were Bible dictionaries! We were witness to the strangest Blooper of all!

(STATION BREAK)

BLUNDERFUL WORLD OF BLOOPERS pauses so that we can meet our guest cartoonist, Bob Dunn.

Bob Dunn for many years has been one of the most widely read King Features syndicated cartoonists. He is also highly regarded among his fellow craftsmen, who have elected him the president of the National Cartoonists Society.

I first met Bob Dunn when he was the featured cartoonist on my "Quick On The Draw" cartoon charade TV program, which I had produced for NBC, the New York Daily News station WPIX, and the Dumont Television Network. Bob Dunn replaced the original TV host of "Quick On The Draw," Rube Goldberg, after his retirement.

As a big fan of my Blooper collection, Bob readily agreed to do a "guest shot" in my **BLUNDERFUL WORLD OF BLOOPERS** book in his inimitable style, for which I am grateful.

Down the Old Mill *Stream*

ANNOUNCER: "Ladies and Gentlemen: Mr. Eddie Playbody
will now pee for you."

It's a Business Doing Pleasure with You

COMMERCIAL: "Ladies who care to drop off their clothes will receive prompt attention."

Fickle Finger of Fate

"Tune in tomorrow and find out if John will goose Sadie's cook, er I mean, will John cook Sadie's goose?"

Air Time

PHIL BAKER: "Name a noisy fruit, like celery."
SAILOR: "—Beans!"

Fit to be Tied

"And just received is a new stock of Reis Sanforized Sport Shirts for men with 15 or 17 necks."

Beauty and the Beast

ANNOUNCER: "And now we present our homely Friend-maker."

Go Go Girl

"Now Marian, if you had your wish, what would you want most?"
"I wanna go to the toilet!"

Quite a Dish

ANNOUNCER: "At Heitman's you will find a variety of fine foods, expertly served by experienced waitresses in appetizing forms."

A Strange Twist

"What did you have for breakfast, son?"
                    COMPLETE SILENCE
"What did you have for breakfast, son?"
                    COMPLETE SILENCE
"Daddy, you're hurting my arm."

Hot Stuff

JIMMY POWERS: "It's a hot night at the Garden, folks, and at ringside I see several ladies in gownless evening straps."

Can-Did Mike

ANNOUNCER: "Ladies, take your fat cans down to the corner butcher."

Game Girl

This charade caused hysteria on the long running Mike Stokey TV "Pantomime Quiz."

AND NOW, AS OUR PROGRAM RESUMES, WE HEAR . . . . . .

Is My Face Red

Tom Snyder, popular late night talk master on NBC-TV, tells of the classic blooper revolving around President Ford. The blooper is bound to get the notoriety of the All Time Great Blooper which centered around President Herbert Hoover, who was introduced as Hoobert Heever. The Daughters of the American Revolution gave a dinner in honor of President Ford. The master of ceremonies of this highly conservative group in attendance introduced the president thus: "Ladies and Gentlemen . . . the president of the United States, Gerald Smith!" There was consternation in the audience when it was recalled that Gerald Smith was one of America's foremost Fascists.

Having a Ball

I was watching "The Merv Griffin Show" and caught two almost simultaneous bloopers! There was a juggler-comedian who was doing his routine, one bit of which involves eating an apple that he is juggling at the same time. He then proceeds to juggle while lying down, explaining that even at home, while sleeping, he never stops juggling. He is at the point in the act he pretends he is at home in bed after a night of juggling in his sleep and says, "And in the morning I wake up with my balls in my hands"—to which Merv Griffin asks a moment later, "Are your balls orange?"

Sick Answer

On the "Hollywood Squares," host Peter Marshall asked player Paul Lynde the following: "You're on a yacht, and you find that you're seasick . . . should you tell your host?" Paul replied, "Let him find out for himself! I've never been sick on a yacht . . . I think you should do everything you can and of course tell the host." The contestant agreed, and Peter said, "Never tell the host!" Paul's reply was short and to the point: "Oh, shit!"

That's Nice . . . Don't Fight

This happened on the game show, "Tattletales." Bert Convy was introducing the three married couples, and he got to John Astin and Patty Duke. He said to Patty, "It's nice to have you," to which Patty replied, "It's nice to have been had!!"

I'd Rather Fight Than Switch

In Los Angeles there are two rival radio stations, KEI-640 and KMPC-710. Geoff Edwards was morning D.J. on KEI; Dick Whittinghill was morning D.J. on KMPC, both 6 A.M. to 9 A.M. They were such competitors that KMPC, owned by Gene Autry, coerced Geoff to come down the street to KMPC to follow Dick from 9 A.M. to 12 noon. Before he would leave the air to do the news on the hour, Geoff used to say "This is Geoff Edwards on KEI, a g-r-e-a-t radio station!" in his youthful voice. Well he moved to KMPC, he blooped, "This is Geoff Edwards on KEI, er . . . KMPC, a g-r-e-a-t radio station!"

Playboy

On "It's Your Bet," Lee Wagner asked Mrs. Cole the following, "What would your reaction be if Michael (her husband) told you he was going on a two-week fishing trip to Alaska with a bunny, er . . . I mean buddy!!"

Enjoy... Enjoy

EMCEE: Before I ask you your first question, Mrs. Robertson, what are you doing in New York?
CONTESTANT: I'm on my honeymoon.
EMCEE: Are you enjoying it?
CONTESTANT: Oh, I'm enjoying every inch of it!

The World's First Blooper

On "The $10,000 Pyramid," the contestant was giving clues on People and Things in fact and fiction. She gave this clue for Adam and Eve! The first two people. Betsy Palmer answered "Edam and Ave."

Does Macy Tell Gimbel?

The TV commercial showed Peak, but carried the sound of Ultrabrite. It showed a tube of Peak toothpaste and said, "How's your love life? Ultrabrite is just dying to know."

Caught Off Base

On the game show "Match Game," a contestant named Chrissy Jones was being interviewed. When asked about her boyfriend she said, "Oh, we ball together er . . . have a ball together."

Heartbreaking

NEWSCASTER: The Senate has confirmed that Henry Kissinger (STATION CUTS TO A COMMERCIAL) is suffering from a severe case of psoriasis.

From Bad to Worse

Heard on KHSL-TV, Chico, California. A man-on-the-street interview with people concerning President Nixon and whether or not he should be impeached. One woman answered, "Yes, because he is the worst thing since our country."

For-Get-It Charlie

On a program called "Operation Entertainment," a female singer sang the song that went like this: "Mike Mike bo bike, banana fanna fo fike, fe fi fo fike, nice to know you Mike."
She was asking the men their names and singing the song. She asked one man his name and he replied, Rich. She sang the song and it went like this: Rich Rich bo bitch . . . . " After that, she asked more names and another guy said his name was Chuck. This time she was a little more cautious and said, "NO WAY!"

Over the Hump

This Blooper occurred on "Hawaii Five-O." Two brothers, who were making a surfing movie, asked about the conditions of the waves. The answer to the question was, "They're humping all over the North Shore." er . . . that is, the waves, of course.

Which End Is Up?

On the "Tonight Show," starring Johnny Carson, Johnny had Donny Osmond on his show. Donny was telling Johnny about his bed, which was suspended in midair. Donny said his workshop was under his bed. Johnny said, "No, you have it wrong, it's the other way around."

Tricky Dick

On "The Newlywed Game," the M.C. asked the wives what was one name that would really get their husbands mad if it was mentioned. One of the wives said that the name would have to be Dick. Everything was okay until she volunteered the information that "That was a sore spot of my husband's!" The audience cracked up and when the wife realized her Freudian slip, she hid her face.

Up Chuck

On "Match Game" some of the celebrities answered the fill-in-the-blank with "throw-up." When the contestant's round was over the camera switched to the host, Gene Rayburn. He turned to the other contestant to tell him that his next question would be "coming up after this message!!"

Betty Baker's Crock Mix

The following occurred on "The Merv Griffin Show": A male guest was talking about his wife's poor cooking, and he blooped, "I bought my wife a new crackpot to cook in." (The audience started to laugh) "I mean crockpot."

Loose Ball

During the Minnesota–Dallas game of the NFL Championship playoff game, Pat Summerall, the sports announcer, came up with this blooper during the first quarter of the game. He said, "Both quarterbacks are not showing their balls, er . . . shy of throwing the balls, er . . . ball."

Finish with a Bang

The Mayor of Statesville, North Carolina, in response to a cannon blast which marked the end of a patriotic program, clearly said, "WHAT THE HELL WAS THAT?"

Food for Thought

The "Tonight Show" host, Johnny Carson, was playing "Stump the Band" with the audience. After the people had stumped the band, he gave them two free tickets. Here is how it went.

Carson: "Here are two free tickets to La Crap, I mean La Crêpe."

Later, after another contestant stumped the band he handed out two more tickets.

Carson: "A dinner for two at Don Peepee, I mean Don Pepe. That's next to La Crap, I mean La Crêpe."

Have You Got a Wrong Number

A blooper occurred on ABC, New York, and was committed by Roger Grimsby at the end of the 6:00 news. Talking about a story concerning a cover-up of a loan for a Salute to Ted Agnew, by the committee to re-elect the President, he inadvertently called it "A Salute to Ted Kennedy!"

Double Entendre

On Johnny Carson's "Tonight Show," during his monologue, someone in the audience called out and asked him if his wife was at the show. Carson replied, "No, she only comes on anniversaries!" Needless to say the audience went wild. Then just several minutes later he was talking about pens, etc., and he quipped, "even his pencil leaks!" Again the audience roared and Carson was beside himself.

Farmer's Daughter

NEWSCASTER: "And here's a local news item. Mrs. Marion Parker of this city, daughter of Fred Parker, who is chairwoman of the County Breeders Association, announced plans for a livestock show. She will show her own cows and heifers and will also show her calves to interested farmers."

Hell to Pay

On the program "Love of Life," the announcer said, "You need all the hell you can give . . . what I mean is . . . you need all the help you can get!"

Paging Mr. Ripley

The following was heard on an episode of "Dragnet." Sergeant Friday was interviewing a swindle victim who said, "I have a wife and three kids, all under twelve."

Breast Feeding

On "The $10,000 Pyramid," Dick Clark said, "Try this delicious breast food every morning . . . that should be breakfast food."

A Part with Teeth in It

On a daytime soap opera, the leading lady of this particular scene was having an argument with a young man and when she was getting to the heavy part her dentures fell. The camera then went on to the young man and he ad libbed a few lines. Then the camera turned back to the lady and she started talking again, and her dentures fell again!! This time the station took no time in putting on a commercial. It was rather funny to see her literally trying to talk with a mouthful of teeth.

A Spare

On the TV show "Bowling for Dollars," host Bob Murphy asked one of the contestants who in the audience had come to watch him bowl. The contestant replied, "My mother, my father, my sister, brother, my wife, my uncle, and my girlfriend."

Beverly Hillbilly

Dinah Shore had opera singer Beverly Sills as her guest. Dinah blooped; I wish to thank a great talent for appearing on my show . . .Beverly Hills. . .I mean Sopera star Beverly Sills!"

Oh, Nuts

Hank Stram, Kansas City Chiefs' head football coach, said to a TV interviewer: "After all, where would our team be without their supporters?"

Top That

A sports director at WSIP in Pointsville, Kentucky has a one hour easy listening show called The Record Shop. Occasionally he plays a record that is very much upbeat from the Top-40 list and usually identifies it as such on the air. Well, one afternoon, it went something like this: ". . . and now let's listen to another of the more popular records from the Top-Farty Chort."

A Shot in the Dark

Heard on CKXH, Calgary, Alberta, Canada—"One man armed with a shawed-off sot gun, shawed-off sotgun (pause) short arm shot gun . . . sawed-off shotgun!"

Just Ducky

Bob Ruby, WWL Radio, uttered this short but memorable remark: "And now, here's the Channel 6 weatherman . . . I beg your pardon, the Channel 4 weatherman, Al Duckworth."

When You Gotta Go, You Gotta Go

On the popular TV show "Three on a Match," a lady contestant very excitedly asked to be excused when it came to her final question, because "nature calls." Bill Cullen asked if she could wait till after the commercial. (Audience roared)

Knock Out

Back in the much more broadcast-conservative late 50s, Steve Allen introduced a female guest vocalist's performance as follows: "I like the way she gets out there and socks out a song. She's not like those who just go and hang out there!!! "Now don't get me wrong, I'm not knocking the hangers, and I guess I'm not hanging the knockers."

He Stepped in It

COMMERCIAL: "For the best in foot comfort buy Triple Shitty Shoes . . . Triple City Shoes."

I'm Susan, Flu Me!

ABC's Bill Beutel was talking about the flu season and he blooped, "The flee Susan . . . flu Susan . . . Flu *Season!*"

Big Deal

On "The Mike Douglas Show," Mike and Dyan Cannon were discussing what kind of men attracted her. She explained that she had once preferred chasing men who were "hard to get," but that now she much more enjoyed an open, straightforward type of guy. Mike commented that he found that a typical modern sexual attitude, and added, "It used to be that you couldn't touch some girls with a ten-foot pole. Well, I was the guy with the twelve-foot pole." (BRIEF PAUSE AND AUDIENCE SNICKERS) "Oh . . . this audience!"

Sky High

Just before the hockey game between the New York Rangers and the Buffalo Sabres in Buffalo, the National Anthems of both Canada and the United States were played. The Canadian National Anthem was suddenly interrupted with a commercial for Eastern Airlines. As soon as the ad was completed, live action was resumed just in time for the final half line of the National Anthem of the United States.

Knocked Up

A gal on TV was shown for the March of Dimes. She knocked on one door and when the lady answered she said, "Good afternoon, I'm collecting for the knockers . . . I mean Mother's March to help fight against Birth Control . . . Birth Defects."

Safety First

On WLS in Chicago the announcer said, "For all you streakers out in the Chicago land area, put on your rubbers (pause) because it's going to rain tonight."

He's Pooped

DISC JOCKEY: "Check your local newspooper for movie listings."

Frogman

Alan Kasper described the weather for New York on CBS. He said, "Besides the freezing rain, watch out for the *spread of Fred.*" He then corrected himself and said, "that should be spread of frog, er . . . fog!!" He then admittedly said, "My words aren't coming out too good tonight."

A Red-Faced Announcer

The following was heard at the end of the Waltons: "See tomorrow night's virgin of Little Red Riding Hood on this channel."

Dear Hearts and Genial People

This happened on KUSC-FM in Los Angeles. "Stay tuned for the oldies show, featuring your *genital* host, Lane Quigley."

Fit To Be Tied

The following occurred on KEYY, in Provo, Utah: "More college basketball scores; West *Vagina* State 69 . . . check that . . . West Virginia State 69. . . . "

Something Smells Here

An announcer on WJR, Detroit, had been playing early Sunday music. During a break he said, off mike, "That was Marshall Wells, our farm editor. Smell that derrière! Er . . . uhh . . . not the French derrière, but DAIRY AIR!"

Wife's Other John

An actress playing a secretary on a soap opera inadvertently transposed the following: "Mr. Coleman is on the seat, will you please have a phone?"

Paging the NAACP

SPORTSCASTER: "Today's football game is just about to get under way, so I now turn you over to NBC's color man, O.J. Simpson."

Hard To Believe

On the ABC Eyewitness News, there was a film clip about the streakings at Brooklyn College. After the clip finished a reporter went on to talk about construction workers who streaked through a building with only their "hard hats" on. The camera then went to the sports reporter who didn't realize he was on the air. He asked if there "was anything else hard." They then cut to another reporter holding his head in his hands in a state of shock.

Sick Religious

When I was interviewed on TV by Atlanta newsman Don Smith, he related this classic. "As a brash youngster fresh out of college, I landed my first big job at a 50,000-watt station in Baltimore . . . WBAL . . . So impressed, I didn't bother to read over the AP copy for a noon newscast . . . I dashed into the newsroom, ripped off a 5 minute summary, dashed back to the studio . . . did the break and hit the lead item cold . . . (obviously some pervert wrote the lead story . . . I read it verbatim). Good afternoon . . . here's the latest news from the WBAL newsroom. Today, crowds of thousands cheered today as Pope Pius 12th stood at his bedroom window in St. Peter's Square and exposed himself."

Shirt Tale

How about the time a newscaster did an AP item cold, and didn't notice the type. It went like this . . . "President Ramon Magsaysay of the Phillipines met the press today. The President was dapperly attired, wearing a gay embroidered shit! (They obviously left out the "R").

Bang-Up Job

ANNOUNCER: "Stay tuned at 11 P.M. when Kenneth Brang-
hart bangs you the news. (Chuckling) . . . my apologies to you,
Kenneth Banghart."

He Ought To Know

A program entitled "The American Love Test" was hosted by
Robert Goulet, Carol Lawrence, and Dr. Joyce Brothers. For the
viewing audience the program posed multiple choice questions
concerning various topics having to do with love in general. One
episode dealt with "How sensual are you?" and covered five questions with four or five possible answers for each. At the very end of
this episode Bob Goulet said, "Now we will tell you how to *score.*"

An Occasional Piece

When I appeared on Jerry Smith's news program on KMSP-TV
Minneapolis–St. Paul in connection with my full length "Pardon
My Blooper" movie, which premiered in the Twin Cities, he told
me of a furniture commercial he did when he described a "three
piss curved sexual," instead of a three piece curved sectional.

Quick Feet

Joe Croghan, Channel 10 Sportscaster in Miami, described a
memorable baseball accomplishment thus: "Lou Brock set a baseball record by stealing first base . . . oops . . . that's a great feat,
if you can do it!"

A Friend in Need

DISC JOCKEY: "Before we continue with our recorded program of music, this word from General Frinance's Fiendly Bob Adams."

Now You See It . . . Now You Don't

ANNOUNCER: "Tonight's Invisible Man will not be seen due to the following Special Program. The Invisible Man will be seen next week. We suggest that you don't miss it if you can."

An Ill Wind

NEWSCASTER: "Tensions ran high in New York City today as thousands of city policemen were on duty to prevent any outbreaks as a result of the visit of Arab Leader Jascha Arafart . . . or should that be Yassir Arafat?"

Green Bay or Bust

SPORTSCASTER: "Well, it looks like the Green Bay Packers are not the shame team . . . same team they were when the great Vince Lombardi was coach. Today they again bit the bust . . . the DUST!"

Hey, Jude

DISC JOCKEY: "Frank Sinatra and Sugar Ray Robinson teamed up to raise money for Danny Thomas' St. Jew's Children's Hospital. I'm awfully sorry—that should be St. Jude's! No disrespect intended . . . but you will have to admit St. Jew is really funny."

Nuts to You

Newsman Larry Glick of WBZ in Boston relates the blooper committed by a fellow news reporter. "Well, the streakers are at it again . . . this time at a local football game just outside of Boston. I can't for the world of me figure out this type of behavior . . . I guess it's their way of showing they're nuts."

Bake Mix Up

ANNOUNCER: "Tonight CBS report brings viewers an in-depth interview with Illinois lawbreaker Howard Baker, who will discuss the Watergreat Bake In."

Friendly Enemies

TV's annual Emmy Award Presentations came up with an unintended blooper. Dick Cavett was given a belated Emmy by the TV academy chairman Jack Cannon. Cavett had refused this Emmy award earlier because it was not announced on the air. In his attempt to rectify the previous injustice, Cannon blooped and said he was now giving Cavett an "enemy award."

Great Poisonalities

Carroll O'Connor, also known as TV's Archie Bunker, appeared on the Dinah Shore Show. He congratulated Dinah on her splendid performance and told her that he was impressed with the famous poisons . . . I mean persons who have appeared on your show.

Blockhead

A sportscaster describing the exciting action of a crucial Miami Dolphin–Baltimore Colts football game, blooped the following: "Johnny Unitas' pass is intercepted by Dick Anderson at the 30, the 40, he is to the Colts 45-yard line and he is getting lots of blacks all over the field . . . blocks!"

Small Talk

Actor David Niven was the host of an Academy Award presentation. The festivities had been moving along normally when viewers at home as well as the black tie audience were shocked to see a nude streaker darting across the stage. Niven, never one to lose his composure, ad libbed, "Let's not pay any attention to him, all he is doing is showing his shortcomings."

He Drew a Blank

An announcer lost a page of his script but gallantly carried on with the following station promos: "What's-his-name is bait for a notorious blank robber Wednesday, on 'Mannix.'"

Good Heavens

COMMENTATOR: "Visitors to London find the city a great
fascination. Sir, where are you from and what is your opinion of
London?" "I'm from Philadelphia in the U.S. . . . I find London
a truly indescribable city . . . especially Westminster Abbey. I
really thought that I was in heaven until I turned and saw my
wife standing by my side."

A Roque by Any Other Name Smells the Same

COMMERCIAL: "So, ladies, remember to add this delicious cheese to your shopping list . . . it's Kraft's roquefart cheese . . . er . . . roquefort cheese by Kraft!"

Ass Backwards

John Cigna of KDKA Radio, Pittsburgh, wanted to say Secretary of Agriculture Butz, but blooped "Secretary of Butts, Butz!"

Do It Yourself

"All the baseball world is talking about Hank Aaron's new home run record, which proves that Hank Aaron, the new Sultan of Swat, could still whack it."

Fit To Be Tied

During the course of a Dodgers and Astros game, Sportscaster Vince Sculley was announcing the results of a Pittsburgh Pirates and Chicago Cubs game. He blooped "Today Pittsburgh beat the Pirates, 6 to 6!"

Is There a Doctor in the House?

ABC's Howard K. Smith blooped: "Dr. Lung said that Mr. Nixon's Lumb collapsed. I mean Dr. Lumb said that Mr. Nixon's lung collapsed."

Jump Suit

During the reports on Evel Knievel's jump across the Snake River Canyon the reporter said, "Even though Evel Knievel has not yet made his jump, preparations for the jump have been long underwear . . . uh, way!"

Oh, Man!

Chris Schenkle, the Sports Reporter, was looking at the Fairways at the Augusta golf course, home of Masters. He gazed at the beautiful trees and said, "Joyce Kilmer must have been thinking about Augusta when she wrote 'Trees,' that beautiful poem and song."

Verree Interesting

On the 10:00 P.M. local news on channel 9 in Kansas City, Missouri, the major news story was the Democratic mini-convention held in Kansas City. One of the news team was interviewing some of the 6,000 members of the public allowed to view the convention in order to obtain their reactions. One of the interviewers unwittingly responded with "Yes, I find the mini-convention very fascinating. I'm a psychiatrist."

Who's Got Pockets

Bob Hope and Jill St. John got cut off the air in one of their early 1950's TV skits because of the following: Jill was playing Bob's wife, and he had his hands tied and she needed the car keys. She went fishing for them in his pocket and gave the line, "Gee Bob, going in your pocket like this I feel a little silly." His response was, "If you go a little lower, you'll feel a little nuts."

What's Up, Doc?

Peter Marshall asked Dom DeLuise, on "The Hollywood Squares," if his lightning rod would work if it were bent. Dom replied that HIS lightning rod wouldn't work. There was some laughter from the audience . . . he said he was going to have his doctor check his bent rod!

Child Bride

The Bob Newhart Show told about his parents coming for Thanksgiving dinner. Several times throughout the show it told how his parents had been married for forty-five years, but within two minutes of the end of it, said that his mother was fifty-six years old. This would mean that she was married at the age of eleven!

She'll Drink to That

Barry Brazeau tells of the time he was working at KVOC in Casper, Wyoming. He was pulling the evening shift. The client on the air was the Tomahawk Room, a local nitery featuring go-go dancers. The bartender called him and requested that he read the following 'live' tag after each of their recorded spots that evening, as business was a little slow. The tag was to read:
"All unescorted ladies visiting the Tomahawk Room tonight will get one free drink."
However, what came out was:
"All unescorted ladies visiting the Tomahawk Room tonight will get one free *dink!*"
By the way, the bartender called him about thirty minutes later to report a tremendous increase in business.

I've Come To See the Wizard

During a live airing of the "Wizard of Oz," the wicked witch is about to subdue Dorothy, Scarecrow, Tinman and the Lion. Dorothy was supposed to say, "The good witch said to call three times and she'd come." However, Dorothy fluffed, "The good witch said to *come* three times and she'd call!

Mama Mia!!!

Radio listeners were jolted out of their seats while listening to WMYQ in Miami. The station was apparently having technical difficulties. The biggest difficulty turned out to be a live mike which picked up this shocker: "Hey, Dave, crank that mother fucker up!"

Take It and Shove It!

"The Flintstones" series had an episode called "Impractical Joker." It's one of those bloopers where the writer put something in the script which he didn't realize had suggestive connotations, and nobody else caught it either. Anyway, Barney is playing this big practical joke on Fred by convincing him that he is becoming a counterfeiter. Barney shows Fred a bunch of bills and says he produced them himself, on a type of paper that is better than the type real money is printed on, and says now all he has to do is spend them all over town to spread them, or "push" them. He says . . . now get this, here it is . . . "I think my money is better than the government's, and I'm going to spend the whole day *shoving it!*"

Freudian Slip?

A network TV quiz show which offered huge prizes for correct answers wanted to protect against any possible scandals such as the one which had involved the $64,000 question in early day television. The announcer in dutifully announced: "The answers to the jackpot question are in the custody of Price, Whitehouse . . . er Price, Watergate . . . I mean Price, Waterhouse!"

Fun and Games

An automobile company sponsored a youth-oriented football contest in cooperation with NFL pro football. In the cities where the pro teams played they conducted what is now an annual Pass, Punt and Kick contest. Various sportscasters had difficulty with this tongue twister phrase. However one who shall remain nameless fumbled the following spoonerism: "And now its time for the annual Piss, Kunt, and Pick event!"

Ain't That Just Grand

On the day Jackie Stewart, the race driver, retired, the Sports announcer on WGN-TV, channel 9, said he won ten "Grand Pees" instead of "grand prixs."

The Moore the Merrier

An actor on the "Tonight Show" pulled this beaut: "This man wrote me and said, 'I saw you in "Oklahoma Crude." You were great. I saw you on "The Tonight Show." You were great. And I think you should be on Mary Tyler Moore!' "

Better Late Than Never

Gene Shalit was doing an Alpo dog food commercial on "The Today Show." He was talking about Alpo. A dog was supposed to eat some before the cameras. But all Mary Lou (the dog) did was sniff it and walk away. Gene said, "The dog usually eats it, but that was one dumb dog!" Later on in the show, while Frank Blair was doing a news report, the whole crew started to break up. Frank chuckled and said, "Mary Lou's eating the Alpo now!"

Let George Do It

The sports announcer on KCRB-TV, Channel 9, in Cedar Rapids, Iowa, when giving the scores of the pro football games, blooped: "George Blanda kicked a 35-year-old field goal!"

Horsing Around

During the course of a NBC press interview with President Nixon telecast on November 17, 1973, a NBC broadcaster finished up by saying, "And we also thank White Horse correspondent. . . !"

Deep in the Heart of Texass

Merv Griffin, after finding out a pretty girl was from Houston, Texas, cooed "I love your *ass*–trode dome!"

X Marks the Spot

Jim Jensen of WCBS in New York, describing that X-rated movies were on a Bonn, West Germany TV Show, said "Seen were appendages from 'Deep Throat!' "

My Secret Love

McLean Stevenson was guest host of "The Tonight Show." One of his guests was Doris Day. He described one of the events that happened when he was trying for a part on her show: "I was in such a hurry to get dressed, I put my foot right through the crotch of my pants. . . . (AUDIENCE ROARS) . . . I did the whole scene that way . . . and Doris, I'll never forget the way you relaxed me (AUDIENCE ROARS)!"

A Bum Wrap

Newscaster: "When the fireman saw that the fire in the lady's house was too large to fight, he went in, raped her in a blanket, and then carried her to safety!"

He Flippered His Lid

Here is a blooper that was aired on RPGE, Page, Arizona. This happened on the "Swap Shop of the Air" program. The announcer said, "Wanted, a cocker spaniel for breeding porpoises . . . I mean purposes."

He Gives Her the Business

The following was heard on the BBC in London: "Princess Anne and Captain Phillips, after the wedding, are going down to the Bahamas on the royal yacht and then go down to South America for some ROYAL BUSINESS!"

No Fault Insurance

The Mutual network carried an auto race. The sportscaster described a minor accident in the race in this manner, "Al Unser in his Sunoco Special just kissed the ass fault in the North turn."

Out of Tune

On WLOA, Braddock, Pennsylvania, an announcer blooped: "Remember, this is the highest priced, low-quality piano on the market!"

Out of This World

Marlon Brando on David Susskind's program: "There's a certain universality of feeling which is almost worldwide!"

Strings n' Things

Mental blackouts on the air aren't uncommon. This announcer had one after playing a Sunday afternoon hour long program featuring the Ralph Ginsberg strings. But he couldn't think of the words, "orchestra," "ensemble," or even "group." This is the way it came out: "You've been listening to the music of Ralph Ginsberg and his string . . . uh . . . his string . . . *bunch!*"

Who Gives a Hoot?

ANNOUNCER: "Music on 'Sunday Classics' today included Mozart's Concerto for Hoot and Flarp . . . Flute and Harp!"

Stop and Go

Announcer Tom Freund of the American Forces Network in Germany some years ago was interviewing Col. John Stapp, called "The Fastest Man on Earth," because he had ridden a rocket-propelled sled more than six hundred miles an hour. Freund said, "Colonel Stoapp, did you suffer any ill effects from traveling so fast and then stapping so suddenly? Uh, well, let me try that again. Did you suffer any ill effects from traveling so fast and then stapping so suddenly? Well, hell, why don't we just forget it?"

Try Lost and Found

SPORTSCASTER: "Oh, yeah! It's a beautiful day for this race about to take place here at . . . where in the hell *are* we anyway?"

I'm Dreaming of a *White* Christmas

NEWSCASTER: "The Metropolitan area is shoveling out after a blanket of dirty snow covers New York Shitty . . ."

The Heave Ho

The young announcer, just hired that day, was given an easy disc-jockey show as a starter. It was called "The Hit Show." The announcer's career at that station lasted for three words. He opened his mike and enthused, "The Shit Ho!"

You Can't Win Em' All

It was after the Joe Louis–Tami Mauriello heavyweight championship fight of some years ago. In the first round Mauriello
charged out of his corner and caught Louis with a roundhouse
right that knocked the Champion across the ring and into the
ropes. Mauriello went after Louis, swinging wildly, thinking he
was about to knock Louis out. Louis recovered quickly and, with
three devastating punches, kayoed Mauriello in the same round.
A few minutes later the fight announcer asked, "What happened,
Tami?" Mauriello bellowed into the microphone: "I'm just an
unlucky sonuvabitch!"

He's Pooped

A newscaster blooping a typographical error in copy he hadn't
bothered to read before going on the air: "And this story from
Blackpoop, England . . . uh, that should be Black*pool!*"

Double Talk

Heard on the American Forces Radio station in Saigon: "Johnny
Ray's recording of 'The Little White Crowd That Clyde' was one
of them that capitulated him to fame."

Happy Sailing

And this unfortunate choice of words from a female radio personality who shall be unnamed: "I was almost late for the broadcast
because I went to see my Uncle Jack off on the Queen Mary."

Nutty As a Fruitcake

The slightly flustered Mistress of Ceremonies was introducing General Anthony C. MacAuliffe on her radio program. The General was famed for his reply of "Nuts!" to a German surrender ultimatum during World War Two. This is the way the introduction went: "Our guest today is a famous soldier, General Anthony C. McNutts!"

Tell It Like It Is

At WDEL-TV, Wilmington, Delaware, a daily women's talk show ended with announcer Bob Darby, off camera, giving a plug for the fashion designer who created the clothing worn by the star of the show. One day Darby finished the show thusly: "Mary Lou Sherwood's dress today by Mainbocher." Then, thinking his mike was off, he clowned: "And Robert Darby's suit off the pipe racks at Robert Hall's."

A House of Ill Repute

The scene, Washington, D. C. The radio studios in the House Office Building. A newscaster was on the air live, but a visitor in the studio thought it was a rehearsal and didn't know the mike was on. The newscaster said, "The House Foreign Relations Committee today began discussion . . ." He was interrupted by the visitor, "Hell no, buddy, that should be House Foreign *Affairs* Committee. The House has *affairs* . . . the Senate has relations! Haw–Haw– Haw!"

Sounds Like Dean Martin

Secretary of State Dean Rusk was being interviewed by several Washington newsmen just after a return from discussions in Moscow. The Secretary was very patient and answered most questions. Then a young reporter, obviously on his first assignment to cover Rusk, asked: "Mr. Secretary, has anyone asked you the whereabouts of Mr. Molotov?" Rusk looked at him and smiled. "No. No one has asked me that question. You may if you want to." A slight pause and the young reporter said, "Well, Sir, where *is* Mr. Molotov?" The Secretary of State said, "I haven't the faintest idea."

Ask Me No Questions . . . I'll Tell You No Lies

A Philadelphia sportscaster was interviewing a baseball player from the Mexican League, whose knowledge of English wasn't what it should have been. After exhausting most of the baseball questions, the sportscaster said: "Well, Jose, what do you do when you're not playing baseball?" "I fock gorls!"

He Needs an Oil Change

The voice of announcer Gil Kreegle, finishing a newscast: "This is Gil Speegle creaking!"

Clean Living

NEWSCASTER: Ageless pitcher Satchell Paige is destined for baseball *immorality* with a spot in the Hall of Fame. Paige said in an interview in Kansas City yesterday . . . "I guess they finally found out I was really worthy."

News Leak

This announcer wasn't sure whether to say look or peek; however, he inadvertly combined the two with the following result: "And time now for us to take a leak at the news."

Fly Me

Heard on "What's My Line?" A female contestant sold silver things. Since nobody on the panel guessed it, M.C. Larry Blyden came out with the following spoonerism: " . . . She makes a silver device for flotting a swy . . . swatting a fly!"

Sound Off

At WLW, Cincinnati in 1948, a radio drama was taking place. The scene was a Middle East market place, and the two principal actors were talking. A sound effects record which was supposed to sound like Middle East background noises was played. The sound effects man accidently grabbed the wrong effect. What startled listeners heard was," "Peanuts, popcorn, crackerjacks, cigars, cigarettes, hot dogs."

Costly Fumble

From Veteran broadcaster Wayne Hyde comes the following: The scene is the Big Ten Football Conference – 1962. Sportscaster: "Harris fades back to pass. He's got Mortenson in the clear . . . nobody near him! Harris throws . . . a beautiful, shoulder-high bullet that hits Mortenson right on the number on his shirt! He's got it! He's . . . the son-of-a-bitch dropped the ball!" (The sportscaster wasn't on the air on the following Saturday!)

And Here They Are!

An announcer doing a promo blooped the following in early 1950. "Comedian Jerry Lester and what's-her-name . . . that big blonde . . . star tonight at eleven on Broadway Open Manhole! . . . er "Broadway Open House" starring Dagmar the gal with the great big . . . smile."

She Blew It!

On "The Kate Smith Show" in 1950 one of her sponsors was Doeskin Tissues. Kate had a way of ad libbing the upcoming commercial plug, and this is what she said: "We'll be right straight back after this word from Doeskin Tissues . . . the very best Kleenex you can buy!"

Some of My Best Friends Do It

Merv Griffin had Mrs. Dean Martin, Mrs. Sammy Davis, Jr., Mrs. Dick Martin and Mrs. Johnny Carson as guests. It was a fashion show and he had all of them dressed in beautiful gowns, furs and jewelry. He said, "Do all you women ever urine . . . yearn for the good old days?"

The Crack of Dawn

A commercial for Rod & Gun Club, American Forces Network, Frankfurt, Germany, extolled the fun of fishing, hunting, skeet shooting. But the soldier announcer just couldn't cope with it at six in the morning and it came out like this: "Like to funt, hish? Sheet scoot?"

Quick on the Draw

Veteran wrestling commentator Al Johnson, himself 270 pounds, was describing the wrestling action from California when one wrestler got thrown from the ring and landed in Al's lap. Johnson (on the air, live): "Get the hell off of me, you sweaty son-of-a-bitch!" Then, remembering he's on the air, "Please watch your language here, sir. We're doing a radio broadcast!"

A Grease Job

The station was WCKY, Cincinnati; a woman giving cooking hints blooped," . . . and then you take a well-greased bedpan . . . BREADPAN!"

Love for Sale

On an early morning man-and-wife show the department store commercial always ended with these words: "Women everywhere will tell you . . . Wyners sell for less!" However, what came out was "Women everywhere will tell you . . . Women sell for less!" (The Program Director of the station promptly reached the victim of the blooper and said: "Get me a redhead!"

Fiddlin' Around

Rock star Bill Haley got his start with a country-and-western group known as the "Saddlemen." Wayne Hyde played the part of an old country character called "Cherokee Henry Hale." One day, Bill had a country square dance fiddler on his show, a good one. "Cherokee Henry Hale" introduced this fiddler, and got into the mood for the square dance and started calling out the dances, ad lib. And carried away by it, he said, in time to the music, "Well, first one bow, second one pass, third one kiss his partner's ass." It just slipped out.

Kissin' Cousin

Veteran News Commentator Truman Bradley, some years ago, blooped "He is a cousident of the President!"

Fired!

KVIN is located in Vinita, Oklahoma, and very little of *anything* ever happens in Vinita, so that when a local fire call is turned in, this is program-interrupting news. The radio station receptionist rushed into the studio with a note which read: "The V.F.D." on way to grass fire at such and such address. Of course, V.F.D. stood for Vinita Fire Department, but Jack Johnson, the chief announcer at that time, slammed the key down and fired off: "We interrupt this program for a special bulletin. The Veterans of Foreign Wars are racing to a grass fire!"

For Shame!

The NBC logo came on the screen, and the voice over said, "This is the CBS television . . . Goddamn it!"

There's Many a Slip Twixt the Cup and the Lip

Anchorman Ron Hunter for Channel 10 in Miami meaning to ask the sports director on the air, how the world Cup Soccer Team was doing, instead asked, "How is the World Cock Sucker team doing? . . . er World Cup Sucker!"

Air Breakers

On "Celebrity Sweepstakes" the question was "What's in the middle of the earth?" A contestant bet on Carol Wayne, who said, "I certainly don't have it, but I guessed gas." (Laughter) A second contestant bet on Vicki Lawrence, who said, "I have gas, too!"

Illegitimate Question

Heard on "Dealer's Choice" Jack Clarke: "Do you have a family?" Female Contestant: "I have a family, but I'm not married." (Audience laughter) Jack Clarke: "Well, you know what she means . . . it happened to me . . . I mean it *could* happen to me!"

An Improviser All the Way

On "The Tonight Show," with Jerry Lewis as guest host, one of his guests was Sharon Farrel, a pretty young actress. In the course of conversation, her new movie came up. She was talking about how her director let the actors improvise during the movie's filming. She was quite impressed by the way the man who played her husband in the movie, John Ryan, used this privilege. "He had such an instrument . . ." Whereupon the audience broke up and Jerry left the stage with all his papers.

Try Milk of Magnesia

On a local radio newscast the announcer said, "Mr. Rodgers, Mr. Payant, and Mr. Bronson constipate . . . er, ah, constitute the committee."

A Sad Tail

A staff announcer for KDKA in Pittsburgh delivered the following news item about an auto accident. He was telling about an accident on a freeway near Pittsburgh. Involved were a woman pedestrian and a moving car. The news story closed off with "The streetwalker was hit in the pissing lane!"

Fingered

On a local newscast there appeared a picture shown on the TV screen of a group of socialites. The newscaster identified them as follows: "Shown are Mr. Jones, Mrs. Brown and Roberts Finger is in her rear."

Ding a Ling

This one resulted in the firing of two persons from television station WSAU-TV in Wisconsin. An "out take" of a spot somehow got on the air instead of the good one. What listeners heard was a spot for a local furniture store in which the sound effects did not come in at the right time. As the announcer finished this take, the phone in the recording studio rang very clearly and as the tape continued to run the announcer said, "Fuck you, you son-of-a-bitching telephone." This is the take that went on the air!

No' Thanks!

Heard on Armed Forces Vietnam (AFVN) radio, "If you think you have VD, go to your nearest medical center for treatment, and get VD free of charge."

He Booted It!

A football game was getting under way when Sportscaster Don Meredith blooped: "And now football fans, it's time for the KISS-OFF!"

A Reverse

A sportscaster announcing a football game blooped: "And there goes O. J. Simple, running a Simpson draw play for a five-yard gain!"

Roll Out the Rug

While I was watching "Dealers' Choice," a man who was selected as a contestant came running upstage and his toupee flew off on camera.

Funny Boner

On the "Jeopardy" TV program, Art Fleming introduced a guest and gave her occupation as an airline tickler agent.

Just Call me Ginny!

A Big Pipeline

ANNOUNCER: "Our 'Want Ads of the Air' continues with this opportunity: Wanted: 100 men to lay Virginia . . . pipeline!"

Man Alive?

NEWSCASTER: "Late dispatches from Belgium advise that doctors are satisfied with the progress in that country's first heart-transplant operation. Reports are sketchy, but we've learned that the recipient is a priest. Actually, neither the donor nor recipient have been identified at this time, but doctors report that both are in fine condition and resting comfortably."

The Big Lie

On an educational TV show on WPIX in New York City, a teacher was discussing the element of propaganda in advertising and warning his young viewers to be aware of illogical reasoning in this kind of propaganda. He showed an advertisement for Foster-Grant Sunglasses with Raquel Welch as the model.

Teacher: "Here's Raquel Welch. What is she trying to sell? It's sunglasses." He continued: "They (the propaganders) are saying the glasses add something to Raquel Welch. I don't know if she needs anything added to her!"

A Weighty Problem

The following occured on the radio station KYAK, Anchorage, Alaska. There was an announcement of a mother giving birth to a baby weighing 27 lbs., born on August 9th. The announcer went on to say that mother and baby both were doing fine. When he realized he'd blooped, he said, "That should be a baby weighing 9 lbs., born on August 17. We thought mother was doing fine before, now this will make her feel a whole lot better."

Clairvoyant

A KFBC Newscaster blooped: "Funeral arrangements . . . I mean *Final* arrangements are being made in Casper for visitation by Spiro Agnew!"

A Lot of Brass

ANNOUNCER: "The time is now six o'clock . . . stay tuned for Herb Alpert and the Tijuana Brats . . . *Brass!*"

Clap for the Man

Cecil Hale, WFAA, Dallas, was emceeing a spelling bee. A man had misspelled a word. Cecil said, "No, I'm sorry, Sir; that's incorrect."

MAN: "Well, now wait a minute. You've been asking us to spell words How about you spelling one for us?"

HALE: "Be glad to if I can. What's the word?"

MAN: "Spell 'gonorrhea' ?"

HALE: "G-O-N-D-O-L-I-E-R. Gondolier. Thank you very much, Sir!

(WFAA Dallas Radio gave Hale a fifteen-dollar-a-week raise for thinking on his feet). At that time, fifteen dollars was a considerable raise.

Good Show!

Here's one heard on a Canadian Broadcasting Corporation, news broadcast when the British royal family toured British Columbia during it's centennial year. CBC announcer Lamont Telden was covering the arrival of the royal plane in Vancouver and he said: "The door's opening. There's the Queen, Prince Phillip and Princess Anne." There was a pause for crowd clapping and then Lamont said, "Princess Phillip waves."

Boy What a Pair!

A novice radio announcer on KBLW radio, Logan, Utah, made this double blooper. "It's 5:15 in Bridgeland, we'll take a look at the Utah Nudes at 5:30, but right now music continues with the Harper's Brasierre. YIPE! Utah *News* . . . Harper's *Bazaar!*"

Giff Goof

ANNOUNCER: "This is Frank Gifford saying, 'Compare all the features and you'll buy Westinghouse' (cut in) 'See all the Zenith models at Ray's TV!' "

Can't Get a Curse Word in Edgewise

A Blooper was heard on the Monday Night Football game on ABC. A mike had apparently been placed on the Chicago Bear Coach, Abe Gibron. It occurred on the first penalty of the game, which was against the Bears. After the whistle blew, a "Goddamn it!" came over the air. Howard Cosell was so busy talking, as usual, he made no reference to the remark.

Life Is Just a Bowl of Cherries!

When the "Tonight Show" originates in Hollywood, an attractive girl usually comes out following Johnny Carson's monologue. On one show a well-stacked blonde came on stage wearing hot pants, and a crossover bikini-type top, highlighted by an ornament of false cherries as a centerpiece. After the usual what's-your-name, what-do-you-dos, Carson looked down at the piece of jewelry . . . Carson: "I like your trinkets!" (audience laughter) "Come on! It's a little group of cherries!" (more laughter) "Well, you just don't see a group of cherries all the time!" (audience roars).

Letter Perfect

When the Kay Jewelry Company was one of the main businesses on North High Street in Columbus, Ohio, a radio announcer gave an appealing commercial to visit the store during their Diamond Sale. He ended with "You, too, can wear diamonds, *if you see Kay!*"

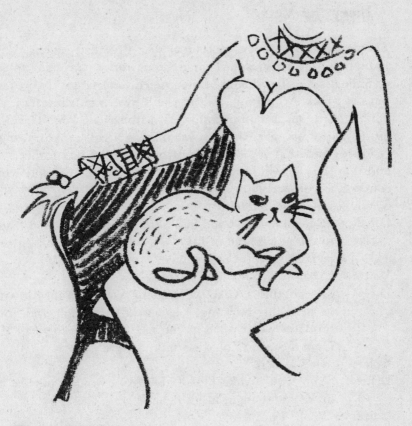

The Cat's Meow

On the "Johnny Carson Show," Zsa Zsa Gabor guest-starred. She was sitting with a cat in her lap when she said, "Johnny, would you like to pet my pussy?" Johnny reportedly said, "Sure, if you move that damn cat out of the way!'

'Tain't Funny

NEWSCASTER: "After the girl was killed, it appeared she was sexually amused . . . I mean sexually abused!"

Bleep the Veep!

The day following the resignation of Vice-President Agnew, radio station 13Q in Pittsburgh, Pennyslvania, ran a straw poll to see who the listeners felt should be nominated as successor. In contention was Jack Armstrong, that station's own night time D.J. At 9:30 A.M. it was announced that Armstrong had won. The D.J. on the air, announced that he was placing a call to Armstrong's residence and that he knew Armstrong went to bed rather late and that the call would surely get him out of bed. The following conversation ensued:

Sleepy female voice: "Hello?"

D.J.: "I'm sorry but if you had answered the phone "I listen to the new sound of 13Q, you'd have won our cash call jackpot. Is this Peggy?"

Voice: "Yeah."

D.J.: "Peggy, this is Mike over at 13Q. You're on the air with us here this morning. We had a straw poll and your husband was elected as the next Vice-President of the United States. Could we talk to Jack?"

Voice: "He's asleep."

D.J.: "You won't wake him, huh? Well, would you like to make a statement in his behalf?"

Voice: "Yeah! Fuck Off!"

Fade to commercial.

Come Now

Newsman Tom Decker announced that, "Russian spacemen were experimenting in growing their own food in outer space, and are harvesting several microorgasms!"

Fanny Girl

ANNOUNCER: "Stay tuned for "People Are Fanny!"

Up Tight

On TV's "Pro Bowlers Tour," the M.C. was talking about one of the bowlers and said, "This boy has been in tighter S-H-I-Tua-tions than this!"

Congratulations

It was a lazy Sunday afternoon, around Christmastime, and KKTV, the CBS outlet for Colorado Springs, Colorado, was doing a local simulcast of "The Messiah," presented by the Music Department of Colorado College in Colorado Springs. Up in the control room, in the radio end of things a young announcer sat on stand-by. He was listening to the music and daydreaming when suddenly he realized "The Messiah" was over and that he had no fill music cued for the turntable. He cut his microphone on and gave the call letters of the station. Then he shut his microphone off and bolted for the record room just behind the control room. He grabbed the first general service that came to hand. He bounded back into the control room, cued the record on the turn-table and cut the whole thing back on the air. Listeners at home heard "The Messiah" come to an end, a pause, the call letters of the station, another pause, and then the strains of an orchestrated version of "Happy Birthday to You" wafted out over the air waves!

Bargain Day

On WJW-TV in Cleveland they were showing the movie, "Cry Rape!" A scene showed a young girl who came to her husband and said, "Honey, I was just raped! (They then cut to a commercial) "at a Sears and Roebuck Store."

Nix

When President Ford arrived at O'Hare International Airport, the loudspeaker voice boomed: "Ladies and gentlemen, the president and Mrs. Nixon."

It Hit the Fan

A novice announcer committed a blooper off the air. Sunday afternoons were deadsville. The announcer-on-duty's chores consisted little more than giving the station breaks, reading the local announcements and seeing that the next CBS program got on the air. Around this time, NBC radio was just starting their "Monitor" weekend offerings, which were hailed as a new concept in radio at that time. The young announcer was so enthused by what he heard that he used some of his free time to write "Monitor" a fan letter. In his letter he told them that he was an announcer for the CBS outlet. He revealed that he stayed tuned to "Monitor" all Sunday afternoons between his stints for the station and that he enjoyed and admired "Monitor" very much. Well, a few Sundays later they read the letter over "Monitor." For the rest of the day, break announcements were gleefully given, such as: "This is "Monitor," where CBS announcers listen most!!!" The young announcer was promptly terminated.

Running Back

A sports announcer on WCVL came up with this unintended goof. It happened at the time LeRoy Keyes was playing for Purdue and it was the morning of the annual Purdue-Northwestern game. LeRoy Keyes is black. The announcer opened his sportscast with, "LeRoy Keyes, Purdue's fastest-running black, is expected to be a key factor in today's game against Northwestern!"

Hocus Pocus

The Amazing Kreskin pulled a blooper on channel 5, WNEW, New York City. In speaking of a certain event he announced that it had happened in "New York City, New Jersey."

Dizzy Dean

This went out over the air at WLCL-FM in Lowell, Indiana. Disc Jockey John Wilson reading "cold" UPI Headlines said: "Former White Sox Counsel John Dean again took the witness stand!"

Pelvis Presley

A disc jockey, introducing an Elvis Presley record, meant to say he had sold 300,000,000 disks. However, it came out: "In his lifetime, Elvis has sold over 300,000,000 dicks . . . that is, dicks . . . 300,000,000 dicks." After 3 tries he gave up and played the record.

Fancy Dan

On the CBS Evening News, Dan Rather was telling about the drought in some of the states and that some had received some rain. He went on saying that they didn't know if there was enough to prevent further "crap . . . crop damage!"

Women's Lib

Heard on "Beat the Clock." Contestant: "He may wear the pants, but I tell him when to put them on and take them off."

Biting Remark

On the "$10,000 Pyramid," on CBS, Pat Carroll was giving clues to her partner trying to get the answer, poison ivy. Pat said: "It's that green stuff that gives you hickeys!"

Speak for Yourself

A TV weathergirl told her viewers: "The weatherman has got good news for you skiiers, but bad news for us streetwalkers!"

Time to Retire

NEWSCASTER: "Governor Whitcomb has announced a new fund for Indiana's retarded teachers." The word should have been *retired*.

How Dry I Am

An announcer was doing a remote from one of the small County 4-H Fairs during the summer. That day it was raining badly and he had to do the remote, oddly enough, from the back-end of a station wagon! He blooped: "The next fifteen minutes are brought to you by Sowers dry ass service . . . uh . . . Sowers dry gas service!"

Fark You

A juggler on the Steve Allen Show was about to juggle some eggs when Steve gave this warning to the audience: "You farks . . . uh . . . (audience laughs) . . . yes, farks, you folks in the front can move!"

Yummy

Carol Wayne, an actress who plays the part of the Matinee Lady on Johnny Carson's "Tea Time Movie" satire on the "Tonight Show," was talking about a beer commercial she had done when she told Johnny the following: "I never knew those beer people were so fussy. If your can isn't turned just the right way, they let you know." After the audience stopped laughing, she followed up with this line, "Then they have special stuff they spray on your can to make it look wet and delicious!"

Drafty

Peter Marshall, host of Hollywood Squares, asked one of the stars this question: "In Israel, boys have to go when they are 18. When do girls have to go . . . I mean first feel the draft? (audience laughs) Wait a minute. I meant the draft to go into the army!"

He Didn't Know What Hit Him

A WBZ announcer in Boston made this goof while reading the news: "The man's leg was severed when he was accidentally hit by a subway station!"

As Host He Is the Most

Veteran sportscaster Don Gillis blooped the following announcement during a bowling show he was hosting: "Because of our taping schedule, this show will take place three weeks after you see it!"

Horsin' Around

The Boston patriots used to have a special post-game show on a Worcester UHF station hosted by Cy Vollmer, who came out with the following one evening: "Hello. This is 'The Boston Patriots Hour,' and I'm your horse . . . uh . . . I'm your host, of course, Cy Vollmer!"

Shalom

An announcer fluffed this announcement: "You can win ski equipment and go shaloming down the hill this winter at Lake Placid."

X-Rated

The accidental omission of a letter in a news wire service story can often result in disaster for a newscaster, such as the following: "After her appearance in the movie 'Airport,' distinguished American actress Helen Hayes indicated that she really preferred appearing on Broadway in stag plays!"

Mother Tucker

Veteran Sports announcer Rick Weaver, the voice of the Miami Dolphin Super Bowl Champions, accidently let slip a spoonerism that made radio listeners sit up and wonder if they heard right. He blooped: "The San Francisco 49'ers are having one heck of a time containing the New York Giant's Fucker Trederickson . . . gulp . . . Tucker Frederickson!"

This I Gotta See

During the course of the top-rated "Miss America TV Beauty Pageant" the mistress of ceremonies was telling viewers about the new format for announcing the runners-up and finally the winner. She enthusiastically announced: "I'm sure that all the girls, particularly 'Miss America' will be happy to learn that she will have a new type of climax!"

Skeleton Closet

During an emotional exchange at the Watergate hearings in Washington, between Senator Sam Ervin and Bob Haldeman, Ervin asked: "Do you expect us to believe that you and John Erlichman, two of President Nixon's *closet* advisors, told him nothing about this plan?"

Stinking Fight

Maureen Flaherty of WYSP radio in Philadelphia was giving a brief rundown of the results of the boxing match of the previous night by saying: "His victory was supposed to have been much more impressive than in his last fight against Eugene Cyclone Hart I don't know how many of you are fans of the fart . . . oh my, my . . . that should be fans of the fights."

It's a Pleasure

On the Johnny Carson show with guest host John Davidson, it was announced that his next guest would be Charo. She came out on stage sitting on a donkey. As they were taking the donkey away, she said, "Take care of my ass!"

Garbage Man

On the "Tomorrow Show," Tom Snyder was interviewing a Dr. Stein who had a daughter of average intelligence whom he had trained from birth to become a genius. He had made the statement that his daughter was a genius in comparison with other children of average intelligence only because of the special training he had given her and that any child could become a genius, given this type of training. He said that he had had legal difficulties with school authorities who maintained that too early training of this type was hazardous to a child's development "and all that garbage," (Time for commercial.) Tom Snyder: "Speaking of garbage . . . watch this commercial."

Behind the Mike

Heard on a news broadcast on radio station KCBS, California, Newsman Dave Machelhaten asked their Stock Market reporter, Ray Huchinson, if it was cold in his building that morning, his reply was, "It sure is, in fact, its so cold I've noticed most of the women are keeping their clothes on . . . . coats on."

Fired!

Bill Diehl, doing a radio program on WCCO, Minneapolis, told his audience of a blaze that had just started at a nearby warehouse. He blooped, "fire farters are reported rushing to the scene!"

Two Balls on the Batter

During a baseball game between the Red Sox and the White Sox, at the bottom of the fifth inning the Red Sox catcher was injured. Announcer Ken Coleman blooped, "It looks like a groin injury, but Fisk will stick it out."

Have You Got a Wrong Number!

Back in the old days, WLW radio station in Cincinnati made a practice of playing the National Anthem at the moment of New Year at midnight. At that time the station was running on experimental 500 kilowatt power during the late night period. Here were the mighty five hundred kilowatts pouring from WLW transmitter when the announcer said, "And now our National Anthem . . ." (Brief pause and then from the radio floated the stirring strains of the French Marsellaise . . . Two or three full bars of it with cymbals banging and horns playing away . . . Suddenly a screech of needle on record . . . Total silence for at least a minute . . . Finally, in subdued manner, the opening stanza of the Star-Spangled Banner was heard."

Don't Drink the Water

On the "Jokers Wild" game show on television, the contestant was telling the host of the show about her 7-month-old son learning to swim:

CONTESTANT: "He goes in the pool every day, and he just loves it."

HOST: "Can he really swim?"

CONTESTANT: "Well, you can see him piddling around in there."

Sun of a Gun!

The following is a blooper heard on KHOW Radio, Denver, Colorado, by newsman Jim Hinton referring to the Supreme Court decision affecting conviction of Judge Otto Kerner, Hinton reported: "Making him the first federal judge to be convicted while sitting on the beach . . . uh . . . bench."

Hic

In an effort to point up the hazards of driving while intoxicated, the greatest cause of highway accidents on New Year's Eve, Jack Mindy, of WHEN Radio in Syracuse, purposely got drunk on the air. Under the watchful eyes of numerous police officers from the area, he downed two ounces of scotch every half-hour during his 3 to 7 P.M. show. To demonstrate his deteriorating reflexes, a driver education teacher administered various reaction and vision tests, and the policemen gave him frequent Breathalyzer tests. By the end of the program he was well past the point of "disc-jockeying-while-intoxicated," and was far from his normal silvertongued best, when his listeners heard him thank the official guests who participated in the experiment, including Deputy James Sheedy. He said thank you to "Deputy Jim Shitty of the Onondaga County Sheriff's Department."

Doesn't Everybody?

On "The Merv Griffin Show," David Essex, a young rock star from London was Merv's guest. Merv was talking about the song that brought him fame years ago. He suddenly turned his attention to David (who wasn't paying attention) and flashed the song title "I've Got a Lovely Bunch of Coconuts" and David (off guard) replied: "I bet you have."

Big Mistake

John Davidson, substituting for Johnny Carson, was breaking for a commercial: 'We'll return shortly with Jack Sheldon and his elephant JoAnne Worley." (The part cut off was, "and her rabbit)."

Dumb Bunny

Jack Wheller, who has an all-night talk show on KDKA in Pittsburgh, from midnight to 6 A.M., had as a guest, Nancy Cameron, Playboy's Centerfold for the January issue. The listening audience can call the station, make comments, and ask questions. One male caller said that he enjoyed Miss Cameron's spread! Of course, he meant the centerfold spread.

Safety First

Heard on KSMU Radio in Dallas, Texas, ". . . the City Council will meet Monday to discuss the awarding of a condom contract . . . rather condominium contract to . . ."

Tit for Tat

On Match Game '74, where contestants try to match celebrities on fill-in-the-blank questions, a contestant was given this sentence: "When Little Red Riding Hood got to Grandmother's house, she said 'My, what big *blanks* you have.' " The contestant filled in the blank "breasts". There are six celebrities in all and after she matched the first three, emcee Gene Raeburn got to the next celebrity, Fannie Flagg, and blooped "Breasts seems to be the answer, Fannie, let's see yours!"

She Blew It!

The 10,000 Dollar Pyramid is a game show in which celebrities give clues to contestants in order to guess certain things. One topic was "Things put in the mouth, but not eaten." The item was a harmonica. When celebrity, actress, June Lockhart blooped: "It's about four to five inches long and you blow it . . . oh my God! . . . er . . . It plays music!"

Jack Potty

On the NBC quiz show, "Jackpot," the following blooper oc-cured. One contestant was asking another contestant who hap-pened to be a nurse this question: "Which back street became famous for producing Broadway tunes?" Nurse answered: "Bed-pan Alley! . . . I mean Tin Pan Alley!"

Straight from the Horse's Mouth

COMMENTATOR: "Prime Minister Indira Gandhi fell off a horse and cracked a finger Tuesday while riding through an oak forest in northern Simla, her Secretariat reported."

Fumble

About midway through the 1973 N.F.L. season, the New Orleans Saints went on an amazing winning streak. In the beginning of that year the Saints had lost a few games very badly, and even the great Archie Manning had been booed. During the winning streak, John Ferguson of WWL-TV & Radio in New Orleans, asked Archie if the booing had hurt him or his teammates. Archie said "No, I think if was just a small majority of the people."

Plants Have Feelings Too

Heard on the Garden Club of the Air, "Plants, as well as people are made up of tiny orgasms . . ."

Oh, Nurse!

John Chancellor, of NBC-TV, said; "The San Francisco nurses' strike entered its 18th year today."

Takes One to Know One

Heard on a man-on-the-street interview program: "There's two things I hate, bigots and niggers!"

Give the Man a Cigar

Bob Murphy, New York Met announcer, once told his audiences that, ". . . a certain Met was the bouncing father of a proud baby boy!"

He's Got Balls

Announcer Rex Raney, while doing "The Sammy Kaye Sunday Serenade" on WFHG Radio in Briston, Virginia, closed off the program, sponsored by Tickel Brothers Sign Company, in this manner; "So remember, friends, before you buy any sign, test Tickel's first."

Four Score . . .

A sports announcer on WBIR-TV, Knoxville, was given a wrap-up sign while doing the late news sports segment. He continued without acknowledgment of the sign. The cameraman leaned around and whispered loudly, "Just time for the scores." So the announcer swallowed and said, "And finally the ball scores . . . 8 to 4, 5 to 3, 7 to 1, 2 to 0 and a partial score . . . four."

The Old Gray Mare

In the chit-chat between portions of a "folksy" TV news show, a new weather girl commented to the anchorman on Channel 10 of Knoxville, Tennessee, "I'm sure glad to hear about the change in terminology in sports and field events, Carl. I never did like it when they called it 'broad jump.' " Everybody giggled and un-nerved the poor damsel. She fumbled for the forecast and finally muttered, "the biggest factor in the weather is the cold mare's ass that's dropping its load right on our Channel 10 area."

Freudian Slip

An announcer, while doing a station break prior to the religious program "Look Up and Live," inadvertently advised viewers to "Stay tuned for 'Lock Up and Leave.'"

After the Ball Was Over

In a radio sketch many years ago, Bob Hope had singer Frances Langford as his guest. Bob wanted to hock her wedding ring over her objection. They got into an argument when Hope blooped; "OK, Frances, I'll meet you at the pawnshop where you can kiss me under the balls!"

Cherry Picker

The following was heard on a local TV beauty contest; "Is this the night they prick the Dairy princess?"

Dead Men Tell No Tales

NEWSCASTER: "A man and a woman were killed today when a drunk driver smashed into the side of their car. The dead man has decided not to press charges."

Food for Thought

On the ABC Saturday night news, Frank Tomlinson, in describing the Middle East conflict, stated very clearly that "Israel and Cereal" had problems over disengagement, obviously referring to Israel and Syria and the pending negotiations led by Secretary of State Henry Kissinger.

A Hard Time

A Radio D.J., during a public service commercial, blooped: ". . . and so for a healthier hard . . . uh . . . heart contact the Heart Association."

Glub Glub

A Culligan water freshener commercial was presented on Channel 4, NBC, New York. At the end of the commercial the announcer said, "Call your Culligan man, he's under water in the yellow pages."

Yuck!

Heard on the Miss U.S.A. Beauty Pageant, the announcer said: "And the yucky, er, lucky young lady that wins will receive a one thousand dollar scholarship."

Horse Laff

From the 6:00 news on WROC-TV, Rochester, New York, with Ron Robitaille, "Kentucky Derby Winner Cannonade heads a field of 13 golfers—golfers?—horses—that's what it says here . . . in the Preakness coming up this weekend at Pimlico. Very rarely does Arnold Palmer run in that one."

Smile . . . You're on Candid Camera

After giving the 10 o'clock news, the newscaster signed off for the night, but the camera was still played on him. After sitting there for three minutes with a stiff smile on his face he got disgusted, and said, "Oh, shit!"

Now You See It . . . Now You Don't

On WGN-TV, Chicago, a blooper occurred on their afternoon "Garfield Goose" puppet show. Frazier Thomas was on vacation, and his substitute was "Andy Starr" (Bob Bell in the guise of a bespectacled old man). Andy informed the young viewers that after a few commercials, a Mighty Mouse cartoon would be shown. After the commercials, two cartoons were shown, but neither of them was a Mighty Mouse cartoon. But this, however, apparently, had no effect on Andy Starr, for after the cartoons, he enthusiastically croaked, in his old man voice, "Boy, I haven't seen one of them Mighty Mouse cartoons in a long time."

Talking Turkey

This blooper occurred on WFLD-TV (Channel 32). One of the station's resident announcers was Jerry G. Bishop, who frequently cut up, ad-libbed while announcing, and generally goofed around. He introduced the afternoon "Little Rascals" program thusly: "Today, the Little Rascals star in a special Thanksgiving episode, entitled 'Take Your Turkey and Stuff It.' "

Nice Work If You Can Get It

David Frost had Racquel Welch as his guest interviewee. When David received a signal from the control room, he blooped; "Racquel, before I get into you, I must pause for this commercial."

Pisshion Impossible

On "Password," Marty Milner of "Adam 12" and Greg Morris of "Mission: Impossible" were guests. The word was lentil. Greg Morris's first clue was leek. The audience laughed, and the lady contestant didn't guess it. Then Marty Milner's clue was pea.

Nice Trick If You Can Do It

COMMERCIAL: "So if you want to learn how to write, write us for free lessons."

Wet Blanket

Robert Culp on "I Spy" is seen explaining to a girl his chores of a secret agent. "Oh, I do a lot of undercover work," he says. "Oh, don't you men ever think of anything else under the cover?" the girl asks petulantly.

Nasal Drip

COMMERCIAL: "So if you want to get quick relief from the misery of a winter cold, try Dristan Navel Spray in each nostril and you'll feel better in a matter of moments."

Wrong Street

STATION PROMO: "For fun for the entire family see "Sesame Seeds" tonight at six . . . oops . . . Sesame Street!"

Check Me Out

Heard at NASA: "This is the Space Center in Houston with the countdown at ten minus two and still counting. We've just gotten word from the capsule that astronaut Wally Schirra is still in the process of checking out his shit list . . . er . . . check list."

Monkey Business

NEWSCASTER: "The U.S. put a monkey into orbit to test effects of prolonged exposure in space. The purpose of the bio-satellite is to test the effects of weightlessness on a human-size orgasm . . . organism!"

Queen for a Day

D.J. Tom Adams of KUDL, Kansas City, concluded his Dairy Queen commercial with: "You'll find all your other Queen favorites on hand too: cones, shalts and makes, available in parts and quints."

Double Trouble

NEWSCASTER: "There was a power failure today at Norcross Junior High School, resulting in the student body being sent home. School officials told us recently that they expect the power failure to be restored by tomorrow."

Tom, Dick, and Marry

TV and recording star Dick Smothers innocently asked his brother Tom if he'd heard about a mutual girl friend getting married, news that elicits wide-eyed surprise from Tom as he ad-libbed: "No! I didn't even know she was pregnant."

Ass-Tronaut

NEWSCASTER: "Astronaut Alan Shepard will be making the space trip after all, despite major rear surgery . . . EAR surgery . . . that's quite a difference!"

Love for Sale

The following was heard on the N.B.C. game show, "Jackpot:"
GIRL CONTESTANT: "Here is my first clue. First you make
                    the sale, then you open my drawers.
                    What am I?"
MALE CONTESTANT: "A hooker!"
GIRL CONTESTANT: "A cash register—you louse!"

Take Your Pick

When Groucho Marx appeared on the Johnny Carson show, the comedian convulsed audiences with a frank discussion on his marriages. Of one of his wives, Groucho said: "If I came home early she figured I was after something; and if I came home late, she figured I had it."

Plugola

Heard on a D.J. program on Tucson, Arizona's KCUB: "You know, something just happened here that's just amazing! My headphones decided to go on vacation. Through the marvels of electronic engineering, they've decided not to work. So, now I'm moving my plug in and out of the hole and nothing's happening!"

He's Straight Man

During a 'Gator Bowl game between Texas and Auburn, A.B.C. sportscaster Chris Schenkel blooped: "Darryl Royal, now the coach of Texas, once played in the 'Gator Bowl with Oklahoma . . . Oklahoma won the game against North Carolina Straight."

I Liked It Better the First Time

This comes from the political blooper capital of the world—Washington, D.C. An announcer gave the following opening: "This is WTOP in Washington, and we now bring you "Doug's World." Doug Llewelyn will again have some interesting tits for you . . . er, that's tidbits for you."

Chastity Belt

After the usual good-natured boos that follow one of his bad jokes, Johnny Carson retorted, "May a weird holy man tape your sister shut!" After realizing his mistake, he covered up by saying, "So she can't talk, that is!"

Windy

Heard on a weather show in Houston: "This is your TV weather service. The high for today in the mid-fifties, low tonight in the low farties . . . er forties. (flustered) Temperature at the KULF weather station is seventy fart . . . four degrees."

A Lousy Seat

During the commentary preceding the start of the 1974 Astro-Bluebonnet Bowl, Cris Schenkel, one of ABC's commentators for that game, was informing the home audience, "Our sideline commentators will be at . . ." (when the local station cut in with) " . . . the Goodyear test track about one thousand miles from here."

Dirty Crack

On a WCCO, Minneapolis news rundown about a couple of safe-crackers, the announcer blooped: "The safe-crappers were still at large."

The Invisible Man

Heard on the B.B.C. - T.V. London: The announcer said, "Owing to the program disruption, 'The Man That Never Was' will not now be screened."

Humpty Dumpty

A commercial announcer was telling his fellow Americans about the great job his oil company was doing during the oil shortage when he pulled this one: "Yes, America, we expect to be over the hump soon . . . we're pumping harder than ever!"

'T'aint Funny, McGee!

On "Wide World of Sports," the U.S.S.R. gymnastic team was doing its thing. Russian Nicholai Andrionov was at the bar, and he gradually gained speed by turning around and around the bar, attempting to do a "triple flip." It didn't work, and the Soviet athlete ended up flat on his back. Sportscaster Bud Palmer ad-libbed: "The crowd just loves this part of the act!"

Pink Panther

NEWSCASTER: "Police were still searching for fugitive Black Panther Leader, Eldridge Cleavage . . . that should be Eldridge Cleaver. . . . now this message, from Playtex bras. . . ."

The Cat's Meow

A scene from Shakespeare's "Romeo and Juliet" presented on TV is supposed to read like this:

TYBALT: "What woulds't thou have with me?"

MERCUTIO: "Good King of Cats, nothing but one of your nine lives." However the actor's line came out this way:

TYBALT: "What woulds't thou have with me?"

MERCUTIO: "Good King of Live, nothing but one of your nine cats!"

Bank Shot

On the Johnny Carson show, Criswell, a self-styled clairvoyant, predicted that before long, there would be a federally sponsored semen bank, to which all American males would be required to contribute. It was at this point, comedian Bob Newhart got up from his seat near Carson, and jestingly said he had heard enough and that he was leaving. "What for?" quipped Carson. "Are you going to make a night deposit?"

Screwed Up

COMMERCIAL: "So try new Hammer Beverages with new screwy cap . . . . oh . . . I mean screw-on cap!"

Fish Story

Steve Allen to actor Robert Vaughn: "When was the first time in your life you ate a piss of fish?"

A Hard Man Is Good To Find

TV personality, Virginia Graham, had bachelor movie actor, Hugh O'Brien, as her guest. She told him, "The longer you stay single, the harder it gets." When audience laughter subsided, Hugh asked, "Would you mind rephrasing that statement?"

He's Got the Runs

Washington announcer Frank Herzog was broadcasting a Washingtor Bullets-Portland Trail Blazers basketball game. The referee's whistle sounded and Herzog came out with: ". . . and referee Richie Powers called the loose bowel foul on Johnson."

Potty

This blooper occurred during a TV religion class. The nun was talking about someone growing pot in their garden . . . they were caught. A student asked how they were caught, and the nun replied, "It just leaked out; . . . someone just couldn't hold it back."

There He Goes . . . Miss America

On television's "Tattle Tales" game show, the M.C. pulled the wrong card and asked the three male celebrities which one of the three would be most likely to win the bathing suit competition of the Miss America contest.

If You Can't Beat Him. . . . Eat Him

A New York city announcer, describing a plane travel package to different parts of the world, said, ". . . where they put you up in many hotels with gourmet males. . . . er, that is gourmet meals!"

Straighten Up And Fly Right

On one telecast of "The Smothers Brothers Show," a skit involved a man whose zipper was open, as he sat in a restaurant. His date, across the table, tried to tell him, subtly, why he was feeling a draft, but to no avail. She finally blurted out, "your fly is open!" In zipping his fly, the man got the tablecloth caught, dragging it across the restaurant.

A Rose by Any Other Name

One evening, on "The Tonight Show," zoologist Desmond Morris complained that the *Chicago Tribune* had refused to print a review of his book, "The Naked Ape," because of its references to genitalia. Johnny Carson ad-libbed, "You discuss the fact that man is one of the primates. You talked about his penis. What other word could you use for that?" Whereupon Morris pointed out, by way of parallel, that newspapers commonly use the word gun. "They don't mind printing a word describing something that shoots death," he said. "But if it shoots life, they won't have it." Not satisfied with this prudent explicitness, Carson then brought a female impersonator, in an ape's costume, who did a striptease that was not merely questionable, but overly graphic. At one point, a bouquet of flowers sprouted from the ape's crotch.

An Orgy

Allen Ludden blooped the following on "Password." Sally Struthers, Lee Meriwether, and Dick Martin had qualified, with Lee having first choice between Sally and Theresa Merritt. When Lee chose Sally, Allen Luden said, "All right, Sally . . . you play with the lovely Lee and Theresa gets to play with the lovely Dick."

Second Floor—Ladies Lingerie Going Up

Dean Martin's infectious humor hits his guests, charging them up. When Don Rickles appeared on the show, the program was a salacious shambles. Kidding around about a new secretary Martin said he had hired, Rickles added that for her first week's salary, Dino had given the gorgeous new addition to the staff an exquisite nightgown of imported lace. . . . ."The next week her salary was raised," he ad-libbed.

Get the Smelling Salts

The basketball game was between the LaSalle, Illinois Peru Cavaliers and the Downers Grove North Trojans. The announcer from WOGN was obviously nervous, doing what seemed to be his first game. A LaSalle Peru player, Don Slusarek, number 35, was inbounding the ball from the near side of the court. It seemed that the sportscaster had misplaced the roster for a second, and the play-by-play went like this: "Number 35 is going to pass out. He does pass out!"

Bungled It!

On the Rock station WPIX in New York, a D.J. was talking about a record: "And now, the Bungle with . . ." (Song starts, and obviously, the D.J. thought his microphone was off) "Goddammit . . . Jungle!" The song is 'Bungle in the Jungle'. "Oh, Shit!"

Panty Raid

On KFOX, Los Angeles, the newscaster was describing a bank robbery when he blooped: "The robbers cleaned out two girl tellers' drawers!"

After the Balls Are Over

The manager of the Chicago White Sox has predicted that slugger Dick Allen will come out of retirement and break the all-time season home run record. White Sox manager, Chuck Tanner said: ". . . because he likes baseball. In that Atlanta park he will break all kinds of records. The Atlanta park has a low fence and Allen's balls will fly out of there."

Obscene Caller

At WMEY, a local Boston station, an early morning talk show was reviewing the subject of prostitution. One listener phoned in to say, "Joe those — the things they do to the prostitutes can be pretty hairy down there."

Cutting Remark

Johnny Carson's guests are sometimes unwitting foils. Ed Ames, the former lead singer of the Ames Brothers, who left the act and became a TV star, was prevailed upon by Carson to demonstrate his prowess with a tomahawk, a skill acquired during Ames's four year tenure as Mingo in "Daniel Boone." Agreeably, Ames waited while a silhouette of a cowboy, painted on wood was set up. He then let fly with a tomahawk. Although Ames professed to be aiming for the heart, the weapon landed in a spot that prompted the pixyish Carson to crack: "Welcome to 'Frontier Rabbi.'"

Farewell to Arms

Heard on a B.B.C. television program, "Panorama." A police officer said: "I took one arm, my colleague took the other arm. Then we disarmed her."

X-Rated Marks The Spot

One evening on the Johnny Carson show while Sandy Duncan was the guest host, actress Shelley Winters was telling her about sex symbolism. Shelley turned abruptly to Ed McMahon and stated, "Even you're a sex symbol. Do you want me to tell you where?" The audience then roared with laughter before they realized that she meant where in the U.S.— not on his body.

Just a Baby

Ken Roth, newsman for Miami's WIOD, spoke of the death of the famous speed boat racing driver, Gar Wood by saying, "Gar Wood was only ninety-one years old."

Fickle Finger of Fate

This blooper was made by a television newscaster in Sydney, Australia. The topic was the funnel web spider scare on Sydney's north shore. The newscaster's blooper came out thus: "Today, in Sydney's north shore suburb of Pymble, a woman was seriously bitten on the funnel by a finger-web spider."

Come Again?

Johnny Carson is a master of double entendres and his ad lib quips keep the censors on the jump. His opening monologues are masterpieces of shamelessness. As he rides his ruttish range, he flips the blips with such stories as that of the young girl who, after travelling an unfamiliar, cobblestone road on a bicycle says, "I'll never come that way again."

Quick on the Drawers

A Dear Abby letter comes to us from D.P. who writes: "My husband is trying to make me insane. He takes things out of my drawers and hides them on me. I search the house for days. He then puts them back in their place and tells me they were there all the time. How can I tell him to leave my drawers alone?"

Seeing Red

Phil Zinkand was doing a newscast on the all-night show on WWSW in Pittsburgh. The lead story on the UP wire covered the missing daughter of Communist Walter Winchell—" After that blooper he managed to get the word "columnist" in the story at least ten times.

Triar . . . You'll Like It

During a TV adaptation of Robin Hood and his Merry Men, Robin Hood was on stage discussing the whereabouts of Friar Tuck, saying in effect that they were to meet him at that time and place. His henchmen looked off into the distance and in a very clear and impressive voice shouted, "What ho, Robin, yonder comes Triar Fuck now!"

Creamed

COMMERCIAL: So if its delicious fresh tasty ice cream you would like for you and your family, go to your corny grocer . . . that should read corner grocer and ask for Sealtest horny strawberry . . . honey strawberry flavor ice cream!"

Weather or Not

During the rapidly approaching closing minutes of a weather report on the radio, the weatherman blurted, "And here in the Twin Cities the weather floorcast calls for shattered scowers for today followed by flair and partly coolie winds tomorrow."

Take Me Out to the Ball Game

There was some question as to whether or not a "rained out" game was to be aired or not on a local TV station. At the last minute the announcer informed viewers: "The game will be played now that the rain has stopped. We now take you to the baseball stadium for the ballcast of the broad game."

Two Pair and Fair

This blooper was heard during a local weather program in the Twin Cities. The weather forecaster must have had other things on his mind: "The temperature now in the twin titties is twenty-two degrees."

Suits Me

COMMERCIAL: "For the finest in fashion with value in mind come to Barney's Men's Store located on the Magic Mile. This week Barney's having a storewide sale on double knits with fifty percent off. And, fellows, when you stop at Barney's Men's Store be sure to see those beautiful Gabordoon seats."

Climb Every Mountain

Heard on a quiz program:
QUIZMASTER: "And now for twenty silver dollars. Can you tell me where the Urals are located?"
CONTESTANT: "You mean the one that we boys go to?"

All That Glitters Is Not Gold

On a classical music radio station, an announcer was giving his listeners some background information on the composer when he said, "He directed the music for Emperor Eugene's glittering balls during the Second Empire."

Twilight Zone

A disc jockey confessed the reason for this blooper. He had to go to the john very badly and as a result he blooped the introduction to the musical selection "Twilight Time." "It's six o'clock and toilet time."

Fly by Night

COMMERCIAL: "So whether you're flying to Chicago or to Tokyo, fly the best! Fly Northworst Airient Orlines."

Wild and Woolly

WEATHER FORECASTER: "We're going to be having some colder weather tomorrow, dropping down into the low forties, so be sure to pull out your woollies so you don't freeze your things off." (OFF MIKE) "Hey, wait a minute! Who's the clown who prepared this forecast?"

A Timely Piece

A D.J. on WCCB, Clarion, Pennsylvania, caused a few heads to turn when he introduced a song thusly: "From the fifties, a re-release for Bill Haley and the Comets, 'Rock Around the Cock . . . Clock!'"

Snotty Remark

Many bloopers are often the result of announcers running words together. Such was the case of this radio announcer when he gave his pitch for a margerine: "If you think it's butter, but it's snot . . . It's Chiffon!"

Mother Knows Best

COMMERCIAL: "So, mothers, ask your druggist for Bepto Pismol for pest relief of upset stomach. That's Pepso . . . Pepto Bismol for the best upset stomach aches!"

Pucker Up

During a recent hockey game in Boston, this sportscaster became a bit excited and blurted out: ". . . and now Orr catches the puck and rams it between the girlie's legs and scores. . . .of course I meant goalie!"

Working Up an Appetite

COMMERCIAL: "Mama Mia's Pizzeria really cares about your pizza. None of her pizzas are ever prefrozen. All Mama Mia's pizzas are made to odor while you mate . . . wait!"

Take Your Pick

NEWSCASTER: "Officials are still trying to locate two remaining miners trapped in the coal mine. Latest reports have said that the rescruers don't know if they are still dead or if they are still alive."

Time To Retire

NEWSCASTER: "And the search for the missing boy continues with no success. Searching parties consisting of local fire fighters, Boy Scouts, and Civil Defense volunteers are now on their eighth day and no clues to the boy's whereabouts have been discovered. What has caused even further concern is that his father has disclosed to our reporter that he is mentally retired . . . that is the father is mentally retarded and the boy is retired . . . oh, you know what I'm trying to say!"

Bad Break

At a country fair, the judge for a baking contest was about to reveal the winner. One of the winners for the breadmaking catagory was a very attractive young newlywed. The judge had been apparently quite impressed with her physical endowments as well as her baking ability when he announced, "And now I'd like to have you meet the breast bed breaker in the country!"

Hello Dolly

Veteran news commentator Lowell Thomas was telling about the death of Dolly Dimples, the fat lady of the circus who weighed over five hundred pounds and who was the victim of *a fartal heart attack*. Lowell, with his great sense of humor, laughed uncontrollably for the remainder of the newscast.

Boob Tube

Heard on "The Newlywed Game":
BOB EUBANKS: Girls, I want you to listen carefully to this. If your husband placed his hands on your shoulders and said, "Mary, you're a swell girl but your____is too____! How would he complete the sentence?
WIFE: My breasts are too big and they're getting bigger because I'm pregnant. But my husband likes that. My being pregnant, that is!"

Fit To Be Tongue-Tied

COMMERCIAL: "So girls, come on down for the twenty-percent sale on all Playtex bras. Be sure to take advantage of this money-saving sale. Playtex will really give you the correct tit . . . oh, excuse me that's fit!"

Great Suspectations

A newsman came up with this Freudian slip: "Miami Beach experienced two fires in the period of one week. The fires did considerable damage to the plush Algiers Hotel and Carrillon Hotel. Fire Department officials were quoted as saying: "Arson is Expected."

From Bed to Worse

Heard on the "Joker's Wild" game show:
ANNOUNCER: "In addition to yesterday's prizes, Ms. Hooper wins a beautiful ninety-five-foot aluminum Leisurecraft bed and a king-size Beautyrest double-spring boat!"

That's a Novelty

"Stay tuned to 'Television Playhouse' tonight at 9:00 P.M. for an entertaining film entitled 'Something's Got To Give' based on Marion Hargroves' navel."

How Dry I Am

The following was heard on Bob Hope television special: Bob had lovely Rhonda Fleming as his guest. He said: "I really don't know how you girls do it, I mean mud packs at night and sitting under those hot *drivers* all the time."

Out of Bounds

Lou Wood, a newsman on the NBC-TV "Today Show" reported during the Cambodian crisis that; "Rebel insurgents are on the outskirts of California while President Ford played a round of golf with Bob Hope in Cambodia."

Assinine Question

On "What's My Line," Steve Allen and Jayne Meadows appeared as guests panelists who were trying to determine the occupation of a woman who appeared on the show in a telephone pole climber's clothes. Steve's first question: "Might you be a lumber-jackess?"

What's up, Doc?

NEWSCASTER: "Dr. John Emory of this city was killed in a hunting accident on Friday. Dr. Emory, a prominent and respected citizen, left a wife and twelve children. Police say that Emory was mistaken for a rabbit."

Ass Backwards

The dynamic Charo appeared as a guest on the "Tony Orlando Show." In an interview with Charo, Tony said: "You know, this is a great country . . . here we are, both successful even though we are of foreign extraction." To which Charo replied: "You are right, you and I have foreign behinds."

Who Dunit?

ANNOUNCER: "See the Saturday night Mystery Movie on Thursday instead of Friday."

I Get the Point

NEWSCASTER: "George Romney said yesterday that his resignation as Secretary of Housing and Urban Development will come after the November 7th erection . . . that is, he will stick it through the election."

Hobby Lobby

Sometimes one blooper will trigger another such as the time Johnny Carson told his late-night viewers: "You know, the Queen is in town. After the audience snickered, Johnny corrected himself by saying, I mean, the *Queen Elizabeth* is in the lobby . . . I don't know where in the world I've got the lobby . . . I mean, the Los Angeles Hobby . . . I mean, the Los Angeles Harbor."

It Feels So Good

In a TV interview Barbara Eagleton, wife of Vice-Presidential candidate Tom Eagleton of Missouri told viewers that: "Her husband's withdrawal is a great relief."

Simon Says

ANNOUNCER: "See another name in the news being interviewed on 'Meet the press'. This Sunday's guest will be William Simon the President's Fool Advisor . . . that's the President's Energy Cheap Advisor . . . Chief Advisor!"

Homo on the Range

COMMENTATOR: ". . . and from Washington, statistics are showing that more and more men are interested in Homo Economics . . . that is, Home Economics."

Two Chances: Slim and None

Popular Johnny Olsen, who has appeared on more network programs than any other announcer, let one slip when he told "Match Game" viewers on CBS the following: "If you would like to appear in person in the television audience of 'Match Game of '75,' *forget it* . . . I mean, don't forget to write to this address."

Mamma Mia

HOLLYWOOD COMMENTATOR: "It's good news to learn that Danny Kaye has signed to appear in a new musical version of 'Peter Pan' which will be presented on NBC-TV next season. Also appearing with Danny will be Mia Farrow. In the title role, Captain Hooker . . . I'm sorry, Danny Kaye will play Captain Hooker . . . I mean Hook in the new musical virgin of 'Peter Pan.' "

Call Me Madam

"Stay tuned for our movie of the week tonight at 11:00 P.M. Our feature is 'Diary of a Madam' staring Vincent Price . . . that should be the 'Diary of a *Madman*'—that's quite a difference."

Shoot-Out

Dub Taylor, a guest on the "Tonight Show," had been playing with the censors by saying "sh-sh-sh-oot yes" or "sh-sh-sh-oot no" in the appropriate places, replacing the more common but less acceptable word. After he played a song on the harmonica, Johnny said, "Shit, that was good." Fade to commercial with Johnny shouting, "Shoot!!! Shoot!!!" Of course the censors caught it, but if was obvious what he had really said.

Fish Story

ANNOUNCER: "Police suspicion of ex-convicts at a half-way house seem justified when a robbery and murder occur on 'Police Sturgeon' on CBS.'"

So Solly

The program was "Jackpot," a quiz show. It was interrupted by a news bulletin. The announcer said, "This is an NBC News Special Report, North Vietnamese troops have attacked Saigon and South Vietnam has given up. We now return you to our regular program. Unknowingly, the M.C. said: "Oh! I'm so sorry about that!"

Second-Story Man

Johnny Carson was interviewing Shecky Greene, who was telling a story that involved a Filipino bellboy when he accidently said: "Pilliphino." In one of the best and fastest thinking saves, he said: "This guy wasn't Filipino, he was Pilliphino," and continued with the story as if it was meant to be told that way.

Tanks Alot

On WWL Radio in New Orleans after an obviously rough day, Eric Tracy said at the end of a Datsun compact car commercial: ". . . so buy Datsun's 610 Model. This is the luxury-combat! It's also good in combat, folks. They're gonna make a tank out of it so we can win the war."

Dog Eat Dog

Johnny Carson in his monologue told his audience a joke based on a supposedly true newspaper article that said people in the United States might soon start to eat their dogs and cats. The punch line was, "My dog has caught on, I saw him this afternoon burying a plane ticket in the backyard." It got a good bit of laughter and in the middle of it Ed McMahon cut in and said, "Do you know who our first sponsor is tonight?" Johnny said, "Sponsor? No, who?" Ed, "A sponsor who has been with us for twelve years, Alpo Dog Food!"

Liver Boy

Commercial for Amodio Moving Company done by Bob Steele on Station WTIC Connecticut: "Let's face it, two families can liver . . . uh, love better than one . . . live better than one!"

Visiting Privileges

NEWSCASTER: "Mrs. Julie Nixon Eisenhower has decided not to visit a clinic for the mentally retarded in Dubuque, Iowa. Instead she will visit her parents, President and Mrs. Nixon, at their oceanside villa in San Clemente, California."

East Is East and West Is West

The game show was "Blank Check" with Art James the M.C. This show has a segment where the audience participates. Johnny Olsen introduced Jill Ireland and Art James blooped: "Ah, and here's Jill Ireland with that fresh, wholesome, California look. Hi, Jill where are you from?" To which Ms. Ireland replied: "I'm from New York, Art."

About Face

On "Tattletales" Burt Convy blooped, when he asked a question about the International Pies, Inc., fad, . . . "Who would be the better sport? You're walking down the street and POW! you both get a *face* in the kisser!"

Johnny on the "Spot"

Johnny Carson had just introduced Peggy Lee as his next guest and had to go to a station break. After he had cued it, Peggy said to him, "You mean I won't be able to get acquainted first." Johnny, then said, "We'll fool around during the commercial."

Doubting Thomas

On the CBS News Show, veteran newscaster Lowell Thomas blooped: ". . . and President Ford has accepted the resignation of two officials from the Equal *Un*employment Opportunities Omission."

Something Smells Here

Ed McMahon on Johnny Carson's "Tonight Show:" "Now, here's a commercial about a woman who shows why she needs a detoderant, uh, deodorant."

An Orgy

Allen Ludden on his popular "password" program blooped: "Will it be Joyce, Susan, or Jeff who will play with John—the game, that is!"

Sugar Daddy

Paul Lynde always can be counted on to come up with a lulu of an answer on Hollywood Squares. Question: "True or false—was a shipment of 'the pill' really recalled because they were actually sugar pills?" Paul Lynde: "Does that mean that all of the babies born in November will have pimples?"

Winging It

WTOP Channel 9, Washington D.C., announcer Frank Herzog goofed up: "We will bring you the Washington Capitals and the Detroit Wed Rings . . . Wed Wings . . . of course I mean Red Wings!"

Action Line

Heard on Hollywood Squares:
QUESTION: "Were Marines active in the Revolu-
                   tionary War?"
MARTY ALLEN: "If there were Marines around, I'm sure
                   they found a little action!"

Now Hear This!

COMMERCIAL: "For one day only King's Jewelry on Knight Street is offering an earring special for you gals. Mr. King will arrange for you to have your ears pierced *while you wait.* (Off mike) While you wait? How the hell else can a dame have it done . . . leave them?"

Strange Announcer

Bill Tanton, WCMB Baltimore two-way talk sports host, said, "The Texas Strangers . . . uh . . . Rangers were doing poorly in the American League Worst . . . I mean West . . . the way they are playing they look like strangers . . . but they're known as the Texas Rangers."

Jock Itch?

COMMERCIAL: "So go to your coroner grocer . . . er . . . corner grocer and pick up a bar of Dial Deodorant Soap for round the cock protection."

Same to You Fella

The news had just ended, and the six o'clock movie "Up Periscope" was about to begin. The announcer came on the air and blooped, "Now stay tuned for 'Up Your Periscope!' "

Body by Fisher

A radio station announcer made this blooper when announcing the name and location of the station, "In the Golden Fisher of the Tower Building, this is WJR, Detroit," that should be "In the Golden Tower of the Pisher Building, this is WJR, Detroit."

They Got Balls!

The pro bowling tour announcer made this blooper: "Most of the bowlers bring along their wives for caddies. They like to carry their husbands' balls from lane to lane!"

Titillating

Peter Marshall wrestled with the word "abreast" and lost when he asked Spanish entertainer Charo the following question on his "Hollywood Squares" game show: "You and a friend take to the streets on your bikes. Is it all right to be riding abreast?" Charo doesn't have that great a command of the English language, and didn't understand the meaning of the word. Peter finally had to ask, "Do you know what a breast is? I mean do you know what riding abreast is?"

This Isn't Your Life

This was the moment that astonished millions of London's TV viewers. It happened when author Richard Gordon walked out of an episode of "This is Your Life." The incident occurred after Gordon was told by host Eamonn Andrews that he was the star of the show. The author looked startled. Then he retorted: "Oh, balls," and marched off. He vanished behind a screen at the Thames TV studios.

Ducking the Question

On "Match Game '75," they had a question that said, "Since Donald Duck has lost his rating, what has Walt Dissney done with him?" After getting the contestants answer he turned to Dick Martin and said: "What about you, Duck er . . . Dick?"

Baby Talk

This dialogue between William Conrad and Miss Lee Meriweth-er hosting the "Cotton Bowl Festival Parade" who were talking of Texans.

CONRAD: "Well, they do a lot of good."
MERIWETHER: "Yes, they 'do do' a lot."

A Mish Is as Good as a Mile

From Terry L. Withers comes this gem. An announcer doing a promo for Alan Alda's hit TV series about medics in Korea, gave it this inevitable plug: "Tonight, don't mish M*A*S*H . . . miss M*A*S*H!"

Captive Audience

An ABC announcer must have been thinking of Bill Cullen's long association with another network when he announced on a nationwide broadcast for Bill's new ABC game show, "Watch Blankety Blanks," premiering Monday on NBC! . . . er CBS . . . *ABC!*"

Is This the Transylvania Station?

Heard on the closing voice-over of "The Mike Douglas Show" by a KEPR TV announcer: "Guests of "The Mike Douglas Show" stay at Transylvania Warlock Hotel . . . Pennsylvania's Warwick Hotel!"

Parking Peter . . . Er, Meter

On Peter Marshall's "Hollywood Squares," Jim Backus was a guest. Peter asked him, "Can traffic noises affect your sexual prowess?" Backus' reply of "Yes, so you should pull over and park!" caused Peter to flub his re-posing the question thusly: "But, can sexual noises affect your sexual prowess?" Above the hysterical laughter of the audience, Peter could be heard yelling, "Traffic noises! Traffic noises!"

Racy

Let's tune in a sports report on KYTV, Springfield, Missouri: "And today, in the national league pennant rape—uh, race!"

Damn Bandstand

On Dick Clark's "American Bandstand," Clark was doing a live commercial for a new cosmetic. Unfortunately, he picked a wobbly podium to deliver his spiel from, and it fell over sideways, and Clark with it, and innocent ears heard: "Oh, dammit!"

Don't Miss It If You Can

On Allen Ludden's "Password" he gave this rather dubious promo: "I'd like to invite all of you to watch my dear friend Julie Andrews in her new ABC-TV series. It's an hour you will easily forget!"

There's No Place Like Homo

Here's a case in point where an announcer doing a commerical for Kraft Foods in Canada should have chosen his words more carefully when announcing a recipe for a lumberjack sandwich: "When you can't get away to the mountains, enjoy a lumberjack in your own backyard!"

Cockney

A TV program originating in Canada called people from the audience and paid them two dollars for each correct answer to questions. One woman, evidently a cooperative and friendly type, was asked, "What is a sporran?" This would be much more likely to be asked in Canada, where there are more Scottish people. She said, "Well, I know what it is, but I can't define it." The emcee said, "You only have 30 seconds left." "It's that thing all covered with hair that hangs down between a Scotchman's legs!!!"

Boob Tube

Beauty contest winners very often enter the field of television with not much to offer except good looks. Here is one such Miss America, who told millions of viewers, "The crown is now being worn by our new Miss America, who will act as tit . . . titlittle . . . I mean titular leader for all of the contestants from the 48 states."

Shuttle Up Your Mouth

NEWSCASTER: And from Washington comes word that Secretary of State, Henry Kissinger, is soon to journey to Egypt and Israel in another attempt at shittle diplomacy.

Taken By Storm

WEATHER FORECASTER: The weather forecast is a little bit brighter with the good news that Faye is no longer a virgin . . . er . . . tropical storm Faye is no longer a threat to the Virgin Islands.

Right On

SPORTSCASTER: Well the World Series will be under way in just a matter of moments. The military contingent is now making its way to the center field flagpole, where we will hear a rendition of the Star Spangled Banner, sung by Cyril Bloom, as the players of both teams get ready to salute the wed, rite and bue.

Peter's Pickled Pecker

During a radio religious broadcast, the preacher, in trying to describe the personality of the Apostle Peter said, " . . . Peter was an impetuous man, and sometimes said and did things he regretted later. I guess at one time or another, each and everyone of us has had a little bit of Peter in us . . . " The preacher quickly changed the discussion to the Apostle James!

Super Cop

Usually reliable NBC newscaster Tom Brokaw excitedly told TV viewers that "The only thing that saved President Ford from assassination by Sarah Moore was a policeman who diverted the street into the shot."

Behind The Scenes

Veteran newscaster, Walter Cronkite, upon the conclusion of his nightly newscast, leaned back in his chair when he thought he was off camera and almost fell flat on his backside. He regained his composure and closed the show with "And that's the way it almost was!"

A Big Nothing

SPORTSCASTER: The tackle was made by the Chicago Bear's big Bear defensive back Dick Bubkas . . . I mean Butkas of course.

What Kind Of Foolish Am I?

Howard Cosell, whose running off at the mouth has irritated viewers from coast to coast, was strangely silent at the ABC TV telecast of the Kentucky Derby when fellow sportscaster Chick Anderson blooped, "The winner is Prince Thou Art." Foolish Pleasure had just won the race, but nary a word from the loquacious Howard.

Inside Joke

Johnny Carson had Dyan Cannon as his guest on his Tonight Show. He attempted to show his close friendship with the movie actress by telling the audience that he had a "deep, penetrating relationship with her." Needless to say the audience screamed with laughter.

Turn-On

On the 60 Minutes program, featuring Mike Wallace and Morley Safer, a tribute to Judy Garland was presented. A good portion of this mini-special dealt with Judy Garland's drug habits. CBS switchboards lit up with many callers who were amazed and amused at the impropriety of a Nytol sleeping tablet, which followed as a commercial.

I'll Buy That

When a skeptical TV reporter asked how his years of playing ball had prepared him to manage a pro club, Yogi Berra answered, "You can observe a lot just by watching."

It's What's Up Front That Counts

Sammy Davis Jr. hosts Sammy & Company, which features guest celebrities. Adrienne Barbeau, who plays Maude's daughter on the TV Series, wore a very low-cut gown. As she talked to Sammy, he kept staring at this cleavage and asked, "How much of that is real?" When the audience broke up he said, "I mean the character that you play on Maude."

Piano Mover

In a TV appearance, John Browning, noted concert pianist, sat at
the piano and experienced a nightmare. A stage hand had inadvertently set the piano with all the wheels facing the same way. As
the piano kept moving toward the audience, he had to frantically
pull his bench forward to follow it!

Out Of This World

NEWSCASTER: The Russian and American astronauts have
been given the green light for the launching of the Soyez-Apollo
hysterical space fight!"

S.O.S.

On the TV game show, "Gambit," the following Blooper occurred. The emcee read the question, "The name Mae West is used to describe one of the following. Is it an inflatable life raft, an inflatable life jacket or a bra?" The contestant answered, "An inflatable life breast! . . . raft . . . LIFE JACKET!!!"

That's Quite A Difference!

COMMERCIAL: So, ladies, take advantage of this Elizabeth Arden special offer at all Jordan Marsh stores, where you will get V.D. at no extra charge . . . of course I mean Visible Difference.

When You Gotta Go, You Gotta Go!

SPORTSCASTER: Phillips brings his team up to the line of scrimmage with Alexander flanked to the right side. Oh oh, there has been a movement in the line. We're waiting for the referee to tell us which player had the movement.

Handle With Care

In Webster's Dictionary the word "spoonerism" is defined as an unintentional interchange of syllables. A well-known disc jockey was the victim of this tongue twister. "And now we have a new LP by Caravan—that pleasantly insane British group. It is entitled 'Cunning Stunts'."

That's A Lotta Crap!

Veteran newscaster Howard K. Smith reported to viewers about a $100,000,000 crap loss in the midwest flooding.

She's Got Legs

"Our want ads of the air continue with this job opening. The
Monroe Diner has an opening for a part-time party girl . . . that
should be part-time panty girl . . . I beg your pardon, that should
by pantry girl."

Don't Bug Me

COMMERCIAL: Your home deserves a monthly termite inspection, so when you think of pests, think of Chuck O'Hara, your Terminex man.

No Balls And A Strike

Heard on WCAU, Philadelphia: "That's a sharply hit single into the left field and Greg Luzinski hurries over to stop it from going into the gap in left-center. The runner is rounding third and they're waving him on to score! Boone, the Phillies' catcher, braces himself for collision at the plate. It's gonna be close! Oh, no! Schmidt cut off Luzinski's balls . . . BALL!!"

A Marriage Made In Heaven

Heard on an ABC-TV promo for "The Streets of San Francisco": "Stone and Keller pursue a man who marries his widow's cellmate to learn the location of a hidden fortune on "The Streets of San Francisco."

For Pete's Sake!

In a Miami Church service on the air, the guest Evangelist was instructing the congregation in the text material for his sermon, which was to be found in 2nd Peter. As he reached toward his coat pocket to get his glasses, he panicked the audience with, "Let us turn to the book of 2nd glasses as I take my peter out . . ." which was followed immediately by a congregational song, during which the entire congregation tried to regain its composure!

Ups and Downs

COMMERCIAL: Visit our bargain basement—one flight up.

Fly Ball

During a Chicago Cubs baseball game, the cameramen were sin-gling out players who were practicing between innings. They zoomed in on a player on a base, who, in front of millions of people, zipped up his fly, not knowing he was on camera.

A Spell Of Bad Weather

Heard on a KPLR-TV St. Louis weather service announcement: "Today's weather reads partly cloudy with the high around the nineties and the low around the *sickies* . . . sixties!!"

Breast Feeding

On Johnny Carson's Tonight Show, Joey Bishop was guest host. He was trying to guess unusual occupations of audience members. One woman's job was to custom fit bras. When he finally guessed her job he presented her with her prize, "Dinner for four at the breast rest . . . uh . . . best restaurant in town."

Wild, Wild World of Sports

Wide World Of Sports host Jim McKay's overriding problem is breaking in new on-air personalities. Once he counselled a famous lady swimmer-turned-commentator to relax in front of cameras. "Just take it easy," McKay told her. "Like, move in with a low-key question. Maybe about hobbies or something." Next thing McKay knew, the lady commentator had rushed her mike up to a swimmer who split-seconds before had broken a world record. The swimmer was weeping for joy. The commentator shrieked, "WHAT'S YOUR HOBBY?"

Hairy

When actor-comedian Donald O'Connor had a syndicated talk show, he and his guests were discussing hair combing after getting up in the morning. Donald offered this startling information. "I comb my hair in my shorts!"

Quick On The Drawers

Johnny Carson's Tonight Show guest, Red Skelton, came out with this Blooper. He was doing a German baby doctor and he had a baby doll to demonstrate on. He was going to examine the baby's leg. When he found that the doll had nothing on under the robe he came out with this. "Oh, oh, I think we forgot something—no booties!" (The audience cracked up with laughter.)

Planned Parenthood

DISC JOCKEY: And now here's Paul Anka singing "You're Having My Baby" by special request.

Job Wanted

On radio station CJOY, Guelph, Ontario, radio announcer Hugh Bowman was broadcasting the hockey game and in a very excited voice said, "He has the puck and has crossed over the center line. Now he's over the blue line coming up to the goal! He shoots—he . . . hit the fucking goal post!!!" There was dead air on the station for over ten minutes.

Double Trouble

Time limitations in Broadcasting can result in the unexpected, such as two commercials running back to back. An Announcer on WRUF Gainesville, Florida on a Saturday afternoon fell victim to this twosome. "So whatever you do tonight be sure to do it safely. Planned Parenthood is looking for volunteers."

Paar Boiled

Jack Paar, on his late night show, was doing a commercial for a headache remedy. He had trouble removing two of the advertised tablets from their bottle. The audience was amused when he filled the bottle with water, took a swig of it, capped the bottle and put it aside. Twenty minutes later there was a small explosion; pressure generated within the bottle had caused the top to pop off. Paar was understandably startled, and the audience roared.

Don't Knock It Unless You Try It

Johnny Carson interviewed a lady explorer on his Tonight Show. They were talking about elephants. Johnny boldly remarked that he "believed an elephant's penis weighed about 60 pounds." The lady snapped back with, "I wouldn't know."

Turn-On

Merv Griffin had Dody Goodman on the show. She was wearing an overall-type dress. The dress had two large buttons where the straps came to the front of the dress. The buttons were very colorful and kept reflecting his eyes. Merv said, "Those buttons look like channel selectors on a TV. Those are the cutest little knobs I ever saw!"

Illigitimate Remark

A youngster called in to a radio station and won a record album. A disc jockey who ran the program came up with this classic, "I have a sick little kid listening to me who's 12 years old. His name is . . . I can't pronounce it . . . at least his parents know his name . . . that is, if he has parents . . . oops!"

Nuts To You

Joey Bishop was guest-hosting the Tonight Show, and it was announced that Mr. Bishop would once again try his famous occupation—guessing. The house lights came up, and after some hints
from Ed McMahon, who knew all the occupations of the three
previously picked people, Mr. Bishop guessed the first two occupations. Then, he was told that the last occupation was a very
strange one, and that "she does to something what the government does with our money." Bishop knew now that the woman
took something away from something. Then, he was told that it
had something to do with worms. After much wrong guessing, he
finally gave up. He asked her, "All right. What do you do?" She
replied, "I pick worms out of nuts in a nut factory." Bishop then
blooped. "I never knew worms had nuts."

Hair Raising Story

Kay Rogers, CHCL Medley, CFB Gold Lake, had forgotten she
was scheduled to do an evening program. In fact she was washing
her hair when she heard over the radio, "Coming your way in 20
minutes is Kay Rogers with Supper Serenade." Wrapping a towel
around her wet head, she grabbed her daughter's Simon and Garfunkel LP, on which the first cut was the 5 minute long "Bridge
Over Troubled Waters." After a race to the studio, she cued the
record and calmly announced, "CL time 6:33. Here's Guyman
and Sarfuckel and the beautiful 'Fridge Over Bubbled Waters.'"

A Gasser

COMMERCIAL: So remember Ball Park franks! They are
plump when you cook 'em! Immediately following was a commercial which stated, "When your favorite team has lost at the ball
park and you've eaten too many hot dogs . . . try Alka Seltzer for
quick relief."

A Matinee

An announcer for the afternoon movie blooped, "Let's Make Love today at 4:30 . . . of course I mean the Marilyn Monroe movie at 4:30."

That's His Bag

The noted pianist and orchestra leader, Eddie Duchin, was playing at the Essex House in New York, and he was being introduced by the radio announcer at the start of the late night radio programs of dance bands. "And now, may I present Eddie *Duchin* himself—at the piano."

After The Ball Is Over

One of the greatest castastrophes that ever happened to Art Linkletter in public occurred when he was presiding at a very large
dinner in a downtown Los Angeles hotel ballroom for one of the
first coast-to-coast "Emmy" Award programs. He was introduced,
walked out on stage, and just as he said, "Good evening, ladies
and gentlemen," the master light switch exploded and plunged
the hall into darkness. Stagehands began running in all direc-
tions, knocking the entire Grecian set down. Walls, pillars, and
great facades tumbled onto the orchestra. One entire section of
strings was knocked out by an enormous pillar. When the lights
came on again and order was slowly restored, he stood calmly
looking out over the wreckage, and said, "For an encore, ladies
and gentlemen, we will now set fire to Lucille Ball."

Unisex

During an appearance on the "Today" program, actress Betsy
Palmer was called upon to give the scores and highlights of the
preceding day's baseball games. Baseball is a subject to which
Miss Palmer has devoted a minimum of attention. But she went
along without difficulty until she reported that "Minnie Minoso,
the rugged outfielder of the Cleveland Indians, had driven in four
runs with several extra base hits." Miss Palmer, realizing that this
must be an achievement of merit, departed from the script to
exclaim enthusiastically: "Good going, Minnie girl!"

Paging Women's Lib

INTERVIEWER: Our TV guest today is a well-known gyne-
cologist, who is a specialist in women and other diseases.

Labor Pains

Heard on Channel 6 news in Paducah, Kentucky. The Newscaster, Dick Enderwood, was explaining that Kentucky's Governor Julian Carroll's wife "gave birth to a fifteen-year-old girl."

Holding His Own

Freddie Prinze, who plays Chico on "Chico and the Man," also starring Jack Albertson, was telling Dinah Shore about his youth. He was saying how he put on shows in the boys' rest room because of crowded school conditions. He said "That's where all of us boys used to hang out."

I Like Ike

A humorous Blooper was made by Joseph Grew, our ex-ambassador to Japan. It was saved from becoming a disaster by the quick wit of one of the persons concerned. Grew was speaking at a Red Cross luncheon in Washington, which was carried over radio. His topic was selflessness. By way of example he pointed to General Marshall, who had just returned from a grueling trip to China and was due to go off almost immediately to Europe. Nevertheless, he had taken time to come to the luncheon although, said Grew, he had been looking forward to a "week-end in the country with Mrs. Eisenhower." When the dignitaries roared with laughter, Grew realized the slip he had made. To make matters worse, Mrs. Eisenhower was present. As soon as he could be heard, he turned to her and said, "Please forgive me, Mrs. Eisenhower, and please apologize to the General for me." Beaming, Mrs. Eisenhower inquired, "Which General, Mr. Grew?"

Velly Funny

Leading into the eleven o'clock news, Bill Burns, Channel 2, Pittsburg, read . . .

"Hirohito will fly from Washington to New York and Bob Kudzma (weatherman) says there will be a NIP in the air tonight . . ."

Come Again?

Curt Gowdy doing the play-by-play announcing of the first World Series baseball game between the Cinncinati Reds and the Boston Red Sox, was describing the deceptive moves of Red Sox pitcher Luis Tiant. He noted that "Tiant comes from everywhere except between his legs."

Floored

Dinah Shore had rehearsed a song in which she, Bob Cummings and Gale Storm were scheduled to sit together on a bench. Between the last rehearsal and the actual telecast a different bench was substituted—one that, unlike the bench used in rehearsal, had no back. When the number was televised, the three performers sat down, leaned back and disappeared.

Candy Man

Lowell Thomas is rated as one of the all time greats of broadcasting. His more than 40 years as a network news commentator attests to his durability and popularity.

I had the privilege of being invited to his home in Pawling, New York, where on his beautiful farm he had converted one of his barns into a broadcasting studio. I had been a producer of the Colonel Stoopnagle (of Stoopnagle and Bud) Stump Club radio program, and had invited Thomas to appear as a guest. He had such a good time that he extended an invitation to me and my radio staff to play softball against his famous "Nine Old Men" team, consisting of such immortals as Babe Ruth, Gene Sarazen and other luminaries, and in the evening to do our broadcast from his farm. As we sat around in the comfort of his magnificent Dutchess County estate, I learned of his marvelous sense of humor and of his many on-the-air breakups, his delightful but uncontrollable fits of laughter which were usually triggered by something that struck him funny in his copy, such as this memorable news item:

"President Eisenhower visited the chocolate city, Hershey, Pennsylvania, where thirty thousand people greeted him... some with and without nuts."

(UNCONTROLLABLE HYSTERIA)

In Livid Color

On the NBC Johnny Carson Tonight Show, Johnny was introducing the NBC peacock, played by Pat McCormick. "And now, for his last appearance on TV, the NBC cock . . . dropped after 25 years."

This conclues . . . this conclees . . . that is all!!!

INDEX